Praise

'Dr Lisa Turner's model in *Our Conscious Tipping Point* is pivotal for anyone seeking to understand and effect societal change. It's a complex time to be alive, and Lisa's explanation of why is paradigm shifting. All thought leaders and activists should read this.'
— **Dr Joanna Martin**, Author of *Superwoman: Escaping the Myth* and Founder of One Of Many

'This is the book that people need.'
— **Dr Karen Wilson**, GP

'Lisa's insights come across as a brilliant flash of light. She effortlessly synthesises both ancient wisdoms and modern technology. She has keen insights into what's likely to happen in the future. Her writing is an off-the-charts brilliant approach to our survival and humanity. In Kabbalah, the sefirot are the equal to the chakras. The highest is wisdom, which is described as a brilliant flash of light so filled with power and majesty that most people can't grasp it at that level. That's Lisa!'
— **Harlan Kilstein**, Ed.D., Rabbi, Educator, Marketer

'It's no secret that we are in an epic uplevel in our collective consciousness. And there is nobody better to walk you through it than Lisa Turner. The model Lisa shares in this book brilliantly captures the bigger picture and deeper patterns of the massive global transformation we all find ourselves in right now. Even better, she can illuminate the path for you to discover *your* place, role and contribution in the shift. Lisa is a true adept on the magical path, and with her scientist's training and firm grounding in our human world, she connects the dots to bring clarity and light to your next level of power. This is a must-read for leaders in this new time.'

— **Elizabeth Purvis**, CEO and Author of
7-Figure Goddess®: Making The Leap From Six to Seven Figures In Two Years (Or Less)

'*Our Conscious Tipping Point* is a deep dive into the multidimensional realms that influence our life. Lisa has taken thousands of years of ancient wisdom combined with her cutting-edge methods to help humanity return to its highest state and possibilities. This is a gem coming from a down to earth Master with heart.'

— **Satyen Raja**, Founder,
WarriorSage Trainings

'In *Our Conscious Tipping Point*, Dr Lisa Turner adeptly combines science and spirituality to address our current global challenges. Her insights are both profound and practical, making this book a valuable resource for anyone seeking to elevate their consciousness and contribute positively to society.'

— **Karyn Brinkley**, Author and Coach

'In *Our Conscious Tipping Point*, Dr Lisa Turner dives deep into the heart of our collective awakening, offering not just insights but also the suggestion of a practical blueprint for transformation. The journey through this book is deeply reflective, affirming and challenging. It's both uncompromisingly honest and hope-filled, resonating with a purity of love for the Divine. I was taken aback by how accurately the descriptions resonated within me and confounded by the simplicity of some of the concepts. Easy to read, entertaining and pragmatic, the book's impact is amplified by journaling prompts that provide an opportunity for further deepening the reflective calling of this work.'

— **Sharon Strickland-Clark** (PCC, ICF), Leadership and Business Performance Coach, Certified High Flow Coach

'Lisa doesn't tell us how to live, but she does demonstrate and make us think about how we can be, what we can do and how we have more than we may realise for ourselves, our world and the greater good. This book encourages us all to realise our own power and ability to heal. If you are feeling anxious about the future, this book is a concept to help gather thoughts and hope – to feel safer and prepared.'

— **Rachel Sampson**, Facilitator and Coach

'This book appeared at the perfect time and Lisa's writing has filled me with so much hope for the present and future and I am extremely thankful

to have read it. The movement towards the crown energy provides a pathway for hope and love to prevail and I look forward to sharing our journey to the conscious tipping point. Thank you for sharing your insight with such clarity and thoughtfulness.'
— **Karen Davis**, Pharmacist and Coach

'If you are interested in spirituality and are a person who loves to learn new things but finds it difficult to find new approaches to what is happening in the world; if you are a person who really appreciates great explanations woven with stories and examples; if you are a person who is also very practical and is grateful when the map is at least half-drawn for your next steps; *and* if you are a person who will be happy to read that you do not need to carry the weight of the whole world alone and you do not need to solve *all* the problems on your own, then read this book!'
— **Silvie Alnas**, Training and Learning Expert, Coach and Consultant

'*Our Conscious Tipping Point* makes sense of the evolution we and society have and are going through. It's a must-read for anyone confused, curious, searching, exploring, expanding and evolving. We hear of the Age of Aquarius: What does this mean? Transcendence: How do we do this? This book will guide you with a practical path and steps for your personal evolution and that of society. The awakening of humanity.'
— **Kathryn Mackellar**, Hypnotherapist, Spiritual Practitioner

Our Conscious Tipping Point

The transcendent awakening of humanity

DR LISA TURNER

R^ethink

First published in Great Britain in 2024
by Rethink Press (www.rethinkpress.com)

© Copyright Dr Lisa Turner

Cover image © Shutterstock | sun ok

For my grandchildren, Elowen and Miriam

Contents

Introduction:
Love Letter To My Reader

D ear Conscious-seeking One,

Are you confused, questioning or possibly even despairing at the world we seem to have created? You're likely drawn to the idea that there is *something* more. Perhaps you use the words spiritual, conscious or soul to describe this *something*.

Do you find yourself worrying about things like the economy, the climate, the environment, patriarchy, misinformation, inequality, bullying and artificial intelligence? Maybe you're concerned about these things but only have the energy to focus on how you're going to pay your bills and make ends meet. Even if you wanted to, maybe you feel powerless to change anything.

Did you once hope that a spiritual awakening would help you, or our world, to cope and change what ails us all, only to be disappointed? Perhaps you have distanced yourselves from some of the beliefs or behaviours of the 'New Age' community. You're not alone. I understand your feelings. A lot is going on in our world, from the most personal challenges to those seemingly unsolvable problems facing us as a species. It can feel overwhelmingly vexing – I get it.

This book is an attempt to put these challenges into some kind of context. Here, I provide an explanation for why we are where we are, and how we got here.

Most of all, my intention for this book is to offer hope. Hope that there *is* a solution, if we can only create it, together. Before we get to the solutions though, we need to explore the true nature of the problem. We need to ask the right questions. We need to avoid making assumptions and dig beneath the surface.

For now, there's something I want you to know. You are brilliant. You are magical. Your light shines so brightly. You are the Divine in human form.

I know you might not feel this right now, and I get it. The challenges in your life might feel as if they are blocking anything beautiful. Maybe you're trying hard to be there for all the people in your life who need you. You're working so hard trying to help yourself or others, all the while feeling swamped with panicked emotions. You may be wondering, 'Can I do it all? Can I help them all? Can I help myself? Can or will anyone help me?'

I want you to know this is not your life – it's just one of the stories of your life. I won't tell you, 'This will pass.' I'm here to assure you that we will *surpass* this.

I used to be an engineer, and the thing about engineers is that they are always asking if there is a better way. They will experiment to 'improve' things (occasionally with hilariously unexpected consequences). Engineers also love models that are simple, easy to use and provide powerful solutions. We like things to work. To be practical. To be useable. This is exactly what you'll discover in this book. A practical model that shows you a way through.

This model, which I call Project THEOSS, elegantly explains how we've gotten to where we are as a Western society and looks forward to what we can expect. It also explains the phenomenon called the 'meta-crisis' (or 'poly-crisis')[1] and how we can transcend it together.

I know you are worried about the future. In my work as a personal and leadership coach and guide, I've worked with many leaders, healers, coaches, mentors and changemakers who want to know how to create a better world and future.

I was brought to this work after being kept as a house prisoner for five years in my teens by a paedophile. I escaped but had PTSD, agoraphobia, social anxiety disorder and deep feelings of worthlessness and depression that affected every waking moment of my life.

Despite being physically free, I was trapped emotionally by trauma. I tried so many therapies, healing modalities and spiritual practices. Despite some progress, I became increasingly disheartened. Some of the therapies seemed to make me feel worse. What's more, they were expensive, painful and tedious. I observed a pattern of two narratives:

1. You can't ever recover. The best you can do is learn to cope with the pain.

2. Just 'let it go' and you'll recover instantly.

I knew deep within my bones that neither was true and there had to be a better way. From that abyss, I realised if the mind can be altered to install trauma, it surely can be altered to heal and initiate growth.

This led me to create Conscious Emotional Transformation (CET) – a modality that turns trauma from a life sentence into a catalyst for profound change without reliving the past pain. CET leverages neuroplasticity and Post-Traumatic Growth Syndrome so that past pain paves the way for unparalleled evolution.

When I first started, I wasn't looking to raise the consciousness of humanity or anything so grandiose. I just wanted to find a way to overcome the limitations of my own mind and what I had been put through as a child. On the way, I found something extraordinary. I discovered not only the solution to healing the cause of emotional pain but also how to resolve spiritual pain.

Though my story is extreme, it is not unique. We all bear scars and hold the potential for rebirth. Although so many are suffering physically, emotionally and spiritually, there is a solution to our individual, and collective, struggles. You can read about those experiences and learn more about the research, the journey, and the results of developing a spiritual technology that enables anyone to be free from their painful past in my other books: *I Loved a Paedophile: The seduction, abduction and liberation of a life*,[2] and *CET Yourself Free: Change your life with the gentle alchemy of Conscious Emotional Transformation*.[3]

As a Western society (and species as a whole), we are in unchartered waters. We are exploring new depths and new territories, so you can stop giving yourself a hard time if you don't know what you're doing. No one does. Not really. All we can do is collectively be ourselves – our vulnerable selves. We can be willing to ask for what we need, to give what we can and to love more deeply than we ever have before.

If you want some help exploring these unchartered territories, you've come to the right place. Remember, map-reading skills are useless if there's no map. What we need are map *charting* skills.

Before closing, I need to clarify something for you, my readers. What I offer is a model. It's an explanation of how things work. All models have limitations, but when we know these limits, we can use the model, confident in its accurate ability to predict or create results. This book will not have all the answers. This work is incomplete and may contain omissions, errors and assumptions that don't hold true in all situations. It is also still useful.

Let's approach this work like a journey, an adventure. All journeys open us to new experiences, insights and information. This book and the models we explore here require us to have an open mind, also known as a 'growth mindset'. It's this mindset that allows us to open up and become receptive to change. To change, I invite you to:

1. Embrace decision and commitment. Decide and commit to your own journey of expansion and exploration.

2. Embrace an attitude of experimentation. As an engineer, my favourite phrase is, 'I wonder what will happen if I try *this*?' This is a phrase that was all too often immediately followed by, 'Oh my. I never thought *that* would happen!' (Said as

I rapidly attempted to turn off whatever it was that I'd turned on.) Sometimes I made a mess. Sometimes I made a masterpiece, but I always learned something, and that's where the true value lies.

3. Invest in yourself and your quest. Reading this short book will take some time energy and attention. You've already paid, so you might as well get your money's worth. There are additional resources, recommended reading and information here: www.OCTPBook.com.

4. Actively seek out mentors, teachers and leaders – those who have been where you are now and are now where you seek to be.

This book speaks about the leaders of the next phase of our human journey. If you're reading this book, you're already one of them. It will likely serve you to find yourself around others who also want to lead our collective, conscious awakening.

Let's keep our eyes on the horizon of the future. It's there. We will find new ways of living and loving. We will never go back to the way things were – we all know those ways were broken. Together we can go forward to the new, creating something different with the knowledge that we can all play a part in our own (re)creation.

Let's explore and chart together, my brilliant, beautiful, divine readers.

1
Patterns In The Chaos

D ear reader, let's start our journey together. Let's begin to understand what might be underneath and going on with all the chaos and problems that we see in the world. Together, we'll find out what has caused our current predicament, and what its purpose might be. Let's find the pattern in the chaos. Hidden within this insane and difficult world are patterns that suggest not that we're on the brink of mutual destruction, but that we are on the brink of a collective conscious awakening. We'll familiarise ourselves with the model known as Project THEOSS.

From someone who tends to avoid predictions, here's one I feel I can make. As a species, we are at our conscious tipping point. We've reached the moment in time and the point in space where the gateway of possible higher-level consciousness is opening for us. As individuals, and as a species, we face a choice: to pass through or not. This is our opportunity to create a conscious future.

As part of Western culture, we used to believe we could control our environment. We felt largely immune to external threats. By 2019, we had cured or protected ourselves against most of the major threats and predators and insulated ourselves from discomfort. Life expectancy had gone up. We had the resources to eradicate hunger, illness and malnutrition (even if we didn't always apply them). As a society, most of us felt safe.

And then, everything changed. Even before the COVID-19 pandemic hit, the signs were clear – not only here, but on a global scale. As a scientist and mathematician, I spot the patterns in the chaos. Project THEOSS explains the waves of world events that have occurred over the last century. It also predicts waves of world events that will occur for the next twenty to thirty generations.

I first created this model over ten years ago, and to date, it has been extraordinarily accurate. That's a *big* statement from this 'once and always' engineer. My confidence in the model comes from this accuracy so far. Looking back at the past 100 years in the Western world, I've observed specific trends in our collective PowerCentre energies. Much like individual chakras,

PowerCentres are powerful energetic flows that can become blocked or excessive, but on a collective scale. When these PowerCentres are blocked or bloated, we experience social change, or 'tipping points'. What feels like our current 'chaos' is an evolutionary catalyst, a sign that we've reached a tipping point where we are invited to evolve to a higher level. We might just be on the eve of the activation of our collective Crown energy. We've reached the top (and final) of our PowerCentres. We are close to the moment when our seven PowerCentres will all be activated.

I will explain more about that in the pages to come, but for now, I want you to know that we are moving towards fully actualised living, both as individuals and as a society. Those creatures who can best adapt are the ones who survive. The same is true of systems. Awakened people know that what happens within the individual is reflected outwards, in society and vice versa. If we choose conscious awakening now, we will create a world of highly evolved, deeply connected people.

Still, Project THEOSS is only a model. It's an explanation of how things work, so let me revise my statement: my prediction isn't a prediction so much as it's an extrapolation. Extrapolation is a fancy word for a straightforward process at the core of what we science and engineering nerds do. We observe events and outcomes, notice patterns and then apply those patterns to the future. We create models. Models are often used for extrapolation. They can be more reliable and empowering than predictions.

Predictions can be fundamentally disempowering, as they can create dangerous self-fulfilling prophesies. If I predict you'll get rich quick and consequently agree to a risky business venture that you'd previously baulked at and end up striking gold... Well, great. If a psychic predicts your current relationship isn't meant to last and then you go home and dump the partner who's made you happy for years... Well, not so great. In my work with clients, they often ask me, 'Lisa, what *will* happen...?' My response? 'Dearest Seeker, what do you *desire*?'

I'm interested in looking *beyond* the literal sense of power. I like to create reliable models. A reliable model can empower us to spot and resolve problems and make breakthroughs, discoveries and updates. Because models can be changemakers, science often likes to be conservative. We like to hedge our bets and avoid promises if we aren't 100% certain we can deliver on them (actually, about 95% is usually enough for engineers to give it a go). We've seen too many broken models, inaccurate maths and faulty hypotheses to get too optimistic. It's beyond embarrassing if the footbridge you design starts to wobble wildly from, well, feet. Cue the badly designed Millennium Bridge over the Thames: those who understood resonance and vibration had a chuckle but mostly felt relief that it hadn't been them on the project.

Science and spirituality are often perceived as being mutually exclusive. Science is based on observing the external world. Spirituality draws its power from the internal experience of observation. Science is *do*-ing. Spirituality is *be*-ing, but we can use both science *and* spirituality. My scientific training helped me pay attention to the nuts and bolts of spiritual programming, the algorithms of enlightenment. In this next section, I want to show you how bringing a scientific basis to spiritual principles helped me to find a working spiritual model. I like to call this the secret science of the psychic.

My 'not so secret' science

We engineers are practical; we're interested in what works rather than elegant theories that have no real-world application. We are used to speaking and describing things in precise and careful ways. That's why we like systems and processes and are particularly fond of models. We especially like models if they work reliably, although we need to know their limits. That's why we challenge assumptions, ask questions of ourselves and others and experiment multiple times. We extrapolate conclusions based on the results of our experiments and observations. We call this the scientific method and we use it to determine whether or not a model is useful. What, you ask, is a model? Great question.

Simply put, a model is something that's used to represent a process, system or mechanism. A common type of model is the scale-model, where a smaller version of the final object is made to test it and find out if it might work. Models can also be mathematical or numerical, where concepts or equations are used to describe a system. The purpose of a model in science is to predict. If it doesn't predict accurately, we first check if we've measured the data correctly by repeating the experiment. If it still doesn't fit, we have to re-evaluate the model.

I adapted this scientific methodology to create models that explain the human condition (why our lives don't always seem to work) and to offer a set of rules to follow or live by to experience a life that does work. Much like an algorithm, I looked for a pattern or listened for an axiom. Then, I extrapolated.

Extrapolation is a mathematical process that involves observing a trend and drawing conclusions or making estimations based on applying that trend beyond the parameters given. For example: if I gave you the number series 2, 4, 6, 8 and asked you what would come next, you would probably say 10. Congratulations, you've spotted a trend (add 2) and extrapolated. This is exactly how I developed these models.

Now, the thing about models is that they are always a little inaccurate. Engineers and scientists know this. We use models and theories to describe what we think might be going on and to explain what we observe.

Each model works differently, providing insights and vast amounts of information on phenomena that we would otherwise be clueless about. Models can be used to explain, explore and understand our world and our experiences. We just need to remember that they have limitations.

So, before we go any further, I'm going to ask you to consider this idea: *it's not about whether something is right or wrong, it's about whether it's useful.* Rather than focusing on binary ideas, truth or falsehood, right or wrong, I invite you to consider this book as a collection of models. The model I'm going to share with you in the next section is no different from the ones in my old lab. It's a model. If the model works (and it does), let's use it. Similarly, you won't hear me saying that what other people believe is wrong – I'm saying that they use a different model. How do you know if a model works? Easy. A model works if it gets results. I like to boil all this down to a simple rule that I call 'Lisa's Law': *'If something works for you, use it.'*

Accepting the concept that all spiritual belief systems are models can be incredibly empowering and liberating. One of the least functional aspects of spirituality is the notion of absolute truths. 'Truth' can be slippery, contingent and divisive (remember, for thousands of years it was a widely accepted 'truth' that the Earth was flat). The way to measure these models is not, 'Are they true?', but rather, 'Do they expand? Do they create opportunities for growth and expansion? Or do they limit and restrict?' Models that enable expansion are probably more useful than those that limit and restrict us. As a species, we are programmed to seek growth to evolve. We question and we seek. This is part of what it is to be human, but it's more than this. It's what it is to be Divine.

If you find something in this book that causes your mind, knowing and experiences to expand (and I hope you do), then please apply and embrace it whole-heartedly. There is no suggestion that these models or beliefs are any better than anything you already have. Your internal expanse is unknowable by anyone other than *you.*

Let's define our terms

To get the most out of my model, it's helpful to understand how I'll be using words or concepts that you might've heard before:

- **Model:** A description of a system and its components that enables us to study its effects and to make predictions about its behaviour.

- **Extrapolation:** The process of estimating or concluding something by assuming that existing trends will continue, or a current method will remain applicable; using facts and observations from what is known to make predictions about what might happen.

- **Energy:** Think of energy as a currency that you or a system uses to do something. Just as you need money to buy things, you need energy to do everything from thinking and moving to making. If you've ever felt too tired to get off the couch, go for a run or even make a decision, that's because your body's energy bank account is running low.

- **Power:** Power is how quickly and efficiently you use your energy. Imagine two people, Janet and Jane, climbing a flight of stairs. If Janet gets to the top faster, she is more powerful. A powerful person is someone who can achieve a lot in a short time.

- **Work:** Work is about achieving something because of applying your energy. Everything you do from lifting a box to writing a book, to cooking a meal requires you to use your energy. We can say someone is doing a lot of work when they are applying their effort or energy to accomplish things and achieve goals.

- **Force:** This is the effort you put into something. If you push a chair across a room, you're applying force to make it move. The harder you push, the greater the force. A person can be described as forceful if they are determined and put a lot of effort into what they're doing. This can be physical, but also mental, creative or emotional effort.

- **Chakra:** Often depicted as spinning wheels or discs of energy located at various points along the spine, from the base to the crown of the head. Each chakra corresponds to specific physical, emotional and spiritual states. Like power stations that manage and distribute your inner energy, each chakra is like a gate that can be opened to let energy flow, or closed to restrict it. When a chakra is open you can access more of the energy type relating to that chakra. You can use this chakra energy more powerfully and efficiently and apply greater force to achieve your goals.

- **PowerCentre:** Whereas chakras usually apply to physical energy centres on the individual, a PowerCentre is a concept I use in Project THEOSS to describe a level of consciousness, similar to an invisible milestone that helps us understand where we are in our collective awareness. PowerCentres relate to our progress in understanding, interacting with and influencing the world around us and within us.

PowerCentres provide a framework for understanding our growth in awareness, wisdom and connection to the broader aspects of existence. They are not physically located in the body but are more about our journey through awareness, understanding and contribution to the world and ourselves. Here's a simplified perspective.

PowerCentres/Chakras

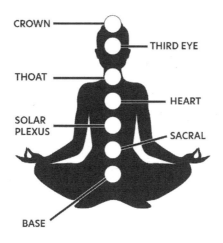

CROWN

THIRD EYE

THOAT

HEART

SOLAR
PLEXUS

SACRAL

BASE

My conscious tipping point

In the opening pages of this book, I briefly mentioned my experience of being kept as a house prisoner of a paedophile and my subsequent search to recover.

I approached my quest like a scientist, delving deeper and deeper into research, searching for a rationale behind what was going on. I experimented with everything and anything, trying to keep an open mind. I studied with shamans, hypnotists and spiritual teachers. I learned reiki, the Kabbalah and NLP coaching, all through to the trainer level. I invested money and time. I felt myself getting closer and closer to real answers. Through my research and experimentation, I found some things that made perfect sense, and they applied well to both the spiritual and the practical. However, others seemed to have some conflicts. Some were confusing. Some were disempowering. I noticed that at times I felt powerful, strong, confident and connected. Then I started to feel fearful. Many teachers suggested that there were a lot of things to be afraid of: psychic attacks, evil spirits, possession, ghosts, hauntings, being overwhelmed by others' emotions... I began to be afraid that what I wanted wasn't what spirit wanted. I was afraid of having no power or control in my life.

I also started to notice how the beautiful, supportive and loving New Age community began to feel judgemental, dogmatic, abusive – even cult-like on occasions. I noticed so many glaring inconsistencies and contradictions. I would have found them hysterically laughable if I hadn't felt that they weren't also dangerous, and even cruel. The message and the teachings that had originally drawn me to these communities were becoming distorted, misused and abused.

As a result, I started to shut down. I started to step away. I became focused on teaching and using my emotional and trauma recovery process, Conscious Emotional Transformation (CET). I avoided using language that referred to 'spirituality' or 'spiritual abilities' – I wanted nothing to do with the toxicity and New Age BS that seemed to have become prevalent.

However, something inside me said, 'You know this can't be right! You know this isn't the way!'

Empowerment

I went right back to the source texts. I peeled back the surface-level thinking and asked myself the uncomfortable questions. I got quiet inside. I listened and I watched as the message unfolded before my eyes. I realised that everything up to now has led to this moment when awakening matters for individuals and society. I realised that we are at a tipping point, not only as individuals but as a species and society. I could see the patterns where evolution had leapt and where it seemed to stagnate. I identified the patterns in the chaos and understood what we each need to do as individuals at this critical time.

I realised there was a system and an order, a sequence that would enable anyone to awaken spiritually, heal deeply and transform profoundly. I realised there was a higher level of spiritual awakening. Conscious awakening. This is what will change ourselves, change our society and heal the planet. I call this system Project THEOSS.

What's in a name?

What does Project THEOSS mean? The word 'Theos' originates from the Greek word for 'God'. You can find the word in the Bible's New Testament. In adapting it for my model, THEOSS stands for: 'The Evolution of the Species and Society'. Although this may be controversial to some, my usage of THEOSS joins divinity to the concept of conscious evolution and change, both as individuals and as a society.

In using the word 'project', I am consciously referencing the two ways this word is used in the English language. One definition of 'project' is an enterprise or series of tasks carefully planned and executed to achieve a particular aim (my background in academia was all about research projects). The second meaning of 'project' is to extend outwards. To cause to move forward (as in, to 'project' one's voice when speaking or singing before a crowd).

Project THEOSS thus does many things simultaneously. It captures both the concept of the Divine and the concept of change over time in the context of a task-oriented process whose ultimate aim is to expand and move forward towards divinity. Linguistically, Project THEOSS names how we, as a species and individuals, are the conscious living embodiment of our divinity. Pretty neat, huh?

Navigating THEOSS: Societal schematics

When we sit down to take stock of humanity, whether we're philosophers, politicians or taxi drivers, we almost always focus on celebrating human progress

('We can whizz around the world in a chair in the sky!' or 'The internet!'), and/or pointing out our major failures (we know what they are). I have a different view. Instead of success and failures, progression and regression, my model explains Western society through *stages of evolution* over (roughly) the last one-and-a-half centuries.

I am not suggesting that humanity did not evolve before the late nineteenth century, nor am I suggesting that our evolution as a species will stop. Instead, Project THEOSS shows a cyclical process of evolution, where each cycle shares something with both past and future cycles. Instead of a straight line of progression with some ups and downs (a model often used by Western historians) or a fixed, repeating circle (a model often used by many indigenous cultures), Project THEOSS imagines human evolution as a spiral.

As we move through our collective past, present and future, each new phase of human existence can be explained by the activation of a PowerCentre.

From chakras to PowerCentres

You've probably heard about chakras or, at the very least, you've likely heard the word 'chakra' before. The word 'chakra' means spinning wheel or disc in Sanskrit. The chakra system originates from India, where it has been used for millennia, and it posits that the human body is made up of seven distinct energy centres called chakras. In English, we call them: the Root Chakra, the Sacral Chakra, the Solar Plexus Chakra, the Heart Chakra, the Throat Chakra, the Third Eye Chakra and the Crown Chakra. Together, they make up a model for understanding emotional and physical wellbeing.

Each chakra is associated with:

- A specific area of the body
- Physical health or diseases relating to certain physical processes, organs or areas of the body
- Psychological qualities and personality traits
- Emotions – both positive and negative
- Spiritual powers
- A colour

In recent decades, the chakra model has become popular with New Age communities around the world. You may be a part of one of these communities. You may have heard of models of spiritual awakening that call for the activation of each chakra. This is sometimes referred to as 'opening' the chakras.

There are many excellent texts on chakras. We're not going to delve into the details of the traditional chakra system here, although I encourage you to explore the topic on your own if you're interested. Instead, I am going to show you how the basics of the chakra model inspired Project THEOSS while pointing out how Project THEOSS can help us awaken collectively.

In my model, I draw on the idea of seven energy centres, each with their distinctive traits, yet fundamentally connected to each other. However, instead of chakras, I use the term PowerCentres. While the chakra model has become synonymous with an individual's physical body and energy system, PowerCentres offer a framework to understand, name and identify where we are in both our collective and individual processes of conscious evolution and awakening. I also wanted to avoid any limitations or restrictions that adhering strictly to the chakra model might present. I'll delve more into the nitty-gritty of how and why 'PowerCentres' in a later chapter.

In the next chapter, I'd like to invite you on a quick journey through our recent past through the lens of Project THEOSS. Project THEOSS illustrates patterns in our collective human history and how they correspond to our societal PowerCentres. My model also describes our current moment and predicts what's to come by mapping out a path of conscious evolution.

Summary

In this chapter, we introduced these insights and concepts:

- **The tipping point:** Humanity currently stands at a tipping point, where we are offered a choice to evolve to a higher consciousness. This tipping point holds profound implications not just for our society, species and even the planet, but for each individual, marking a potential shift towards a more consciously aware future.

- **Models as a tool:** A model is a tool that helps us understand complex systems.

- **Introducing Project THEOSS:** Project THEOSS is a model that explains what has happened in the Western world and suggests a forecast of what might come to be.

- **Challenges of the current era:** Recent global challenges, including the COVID-19 pandemic, have emphasised the urgent need for a shift in consciousness. These events challenge our former sense of safety and control, pushing us to reconsider our approach to a collective existence.

- **Scientific and spiritual synergy:** Science and spirituality might seem at odds, but they can converge and be blended in a way that offers a more integrated, conscious understanding of our existence. This allows us to approach spiritual growth with the same rigour and curiosity we apply to scientific exploration.

- **PowerCentres explained:** PowerCentres offer a framework to understand our collective evolution. Drawing inspiration from the traditional chakra system but applying it to societal transformation, PowerCentres help us navigate our shared path towards higher awareness and connectivity.

SELF-REFLECTION QUESTIONS FOR DEEPER EXPLORATION

1. Reflecting on your life, when have you felt you were at your own tipping point? How did you decide which path to take? Can you draw parallels to humanity's current conscious tipping point as described in the chapter?

2. What are some patterns you have noticed in your life? Do you know the underlying root cause of those patterns or not? How would understanding what is causing repeating patterns help you to make your life better?

3. How do you see your personal evolution contributing to or reflecting the broader shifts in collective consciousness? Are there changes you feel inspired to make in your own life to better align with these shifts?

4. How do you balance your logical mind and your intuition? Do you experience conflict? How have you found ways to reconcile this that have worked? Where do you still struggle to reconcile this conflict?

2

Project THEOSS: Mapping The Milestones Towards Collective Awakening

Now we've started our journey. Our bags are packed with snacks and we have an idea of where we're going. What we need now is a map, and the model, Project THEOSS, is just such a map. This model explains the changes and shifts that have taken place in our culture and suggests a forecast of what might come to be.

Through the lens of Project THEOSS, we uncover the patterns hidden within our past, revealing the profound implications these have for our future. As we surf these waves of change, we'll understand the cycles and gain some clues about where we are headed – together – towards a conscious future.

When we take a look at the last century or so, we can observe a series of events, situations and experiences in each period of our recent history that tend to culminate in a major event that pushes us into social change. These triggers bring us to our 'tipping points'. In this chapter, let's take a closer look at how our recent past lines up with our PowerCentres. This is the core of the Project THEOSS model.

1900–1950s: War and the Base PowerCentre

In the early part of the last century, two world wars and economic depression ravaged the population of the developed world. Food and housing – the basics of survival and security – were in short supply. As a society, we focused on getting food on the table and a roof over our heads. During the 1930s, the Great Depression in the United States plunged the country into unemployment and record levels of poverty and hardship that spread to the rest of the industrialised world. Then came the Second World War, destroying lives and people's homes in Europe. In Britain, rationing lasted until 1954. People were hungry and dwellings were overcrowded. To survive, we had to change. People demanded – and received – reform in the form of a New Deal for the United States, affordable housing, social security, the welfare state and the National Health System in Britain. Encouraged by government assistance, the farming and food industry developed new ways of increasing yield, which resulted in mass-produced, cheaper food. As we passed the mid-point of the twentieth century, most of us had enough to eat, somewhere to live and security for our old age and health care. Thus, our Base PowerCentre of society was activated, characterised by three key personal values:

- Structure

- Security

- Survival

Once our Base PowerCentre was activated, our needs were met, but society tended to be overly focused on rules, conformity and structure. We had to do what we were told. Toe the line. Be good citizens. Behave in the way society expected. When we realised that not all of society's rules served us, we were headed towards a tipping point. Tipping points typically happen like this: a series of micro-changes or events propel us into change.

1960s: Sexual revolution and the Sacral PowerCentre

With the security of knowing that we had somewhere to live, enough food to eat and that we would be supported if we 'failed', it became a little safer to take some risks.

As the conformity of the 1950s began to wear on a new generation, we began to question, experiment and rebel. We rejected the old formula for success: go to school, go to university, get a job, get married, have children… It was too restrictive for young people who desired freedom and pleasure. 'Rebels without a cause' became the hippies and activists of the 1960s who bent and broke society's rules. We recognised that, indeed, some rules had to go. We came together in groups and movements to protest and demand change. We ended legal segregation in the United States and former colonies won independence from their European rulers. A cultural revolution, begun in Britain and the United States, spread across the world, and with it came a sexual revolution. We embraced 'free love'. Sexual freedom beyond the confines of heterosexual marriage slowly moved into the mainstream. Many of the older generations watched in shock as the Baby Boomers, well, boomed. Creativity and free expression and all that came with it – music, art, fashion, sex – flourished. The Sacral PowerCentre of society was activated, nourishing our collective:

- Sexuality
- Creativity
- Pleasure
- Flexibility

In both the United Kingdom and the United States, significant events led to major cultural shifts. Changing ideas around race, class and gender gave rise to protests and social movements focused on addressing class disparities (particularly in the United Kingdom) and ending legal racial segregation in the United States. Across the Western world, women advocated for equal rights. Society became far more accepting, legally and culturally, of different sexual orientations, and old norms governing sexual behaviours were challenged. The working class demanded not only better legal protections but also greater respect. In general, society wanted the freedom to live in more open, equal, inclusive and fun-filled ways, so, as a society, we moved into our Sacral PowerCentre, relishing freedom, solidarity, rule-changing and pleasure.

Stock market crashes and economic downturns signalled the end of our Sacral PowerCentre moment and ushered in our Solar Plexus period.

1970s–1980s: Financial revolution and the Solar Plexus PowerCentre

The 1970s were tough. The United States and many countries in Asia regrouped after a horrific war in Vietnam. Oil prices soared and petrol was scarce. Factories closed and many lost their jobs. Strikes and tensions from workers' unions led to increasing labour unrest. We became disillusioned with a system we began to think of as out of balance. Society no longer wanted to share, or wait. Attitudes changed to, 'I don't want to work until I get a pension and *then* live the life I choose. I want it now.'

With major social changes accomplished (or so we thought), adult Boomers began to focus on striving financially. In the 1980s, a time of financial boom, attitudes towards money and work shifted. Former activist-rebel Boomers now prioritised the individual over the collective. We left formal employment to start our own businesses. During this materialistic decade, we sought to find and create our identities. We tapped into personal willpower to gain control over our lives, work, bodies and finances. This was a generation of 'me', 'I' and instant gratification. Selfishness was a mark of our confidence. Not the community, not society, not the greater good, but *Me*. *I'm* doing well if *I* have the fancy job and the house with a pool because *I* deserve it. No longer satisfied with renting or council houses, homeownership soared and created a housing market boom.

We saw rapid growth in technology (as well as shoulder pads!). Appearance became more important. Madonna released her song 'Material Girl', capturing the essence of the 80s attitude. No need to be ashamed of greed. Margaret Thatcher and Ronald Reagan came to power and the Yuppie generation was born. We activated the Solar Plexus PowerCentre of society:

- Identity
- Individuality

- Power
- Courage
- Willpower

Once again, society focused on the individual: getting a job, keeping a job, earning money and wanting more for ourselves. Government scandals, the excessive power of the unions and high taxes led some of us to believe that we were doing most of the work, yet the spoils were being shared equally (in the company and society at large). Baby Boomers, now well into the workplace and moving up the career ladder, didn't want to share everything they believed they had worked so hard to achieve.

The excessive Solar Plexus PowerCentre finally imploded. We experienced burnout, realising that the money we worked so hard for had brought little real joy, satisfaction or love. We started thinking that there must be more to life than this. We sought connections. Our hearts burst with the love we had been suppressing.

1990s: Compassion and the Heart PowerCentre

After the boom of the 1980s, the 1990s heralded an emotional tipping point. A series of stock market crashes exposed the cracks in a system that promised wealth (and thus happiness) by working hard, working long and buying expensive stuff. We began to experience burnout. As a society, we yearned for more emotional and less material connections. We were tired of the restrictions on feeling and expressing our emotions. We questioned if we could truly rely on logic and numbers.

Disillusioned with their Boomer parents' lifestyle, Gen Xers asked, 'Is money the only thing that matters? There must be more to life than this.' No longer seen as weaknesses, love and compassion infused our world. We touched more, we connected more and we invented the 'group hug'. Kids learned that having self-esteem was more important than having good grades. They got medals for participation ('Everyone's a winner!'). We went to therapy, acupuncture, shamans, healing circles, support groups...

Several key books published in the 1990s planted the seeds of the next wave of the New Age movement. *The Celestine Prophecy* by James Redfield (1993)[4] and *Conversations with God: An uncommon dialogue, Book 1* by Neale Donald Walsch[5] sold millions of copies worldwide. We experienced the rise of the self-help movement with leading figures like Louise Hay, Deepak Chopra and Wayne Dyer urging us to open our hearts to new ideas. The seeds for the next conscious tipping point were planted.

If all this wasn't enough to awaken our emotional centre, the tragic and shocking death of Princess Diana, much loved and newly in love, cracked our hearts wide open with our collective unexpressed grief. The world was in tears. We wept. We felt. The grief we suffered was more than a sign of our love for a stranger in the public eye: it gave us all permission to feel and to show those feelings freely and openly without shame or embarrassment. We opened our Heart PowerCentre, ushering in an age of:

- Love

- Compassion

- Empathy

- Win-Win

- Higher emotions

However, is it possible to be too compassionate? To be too generous and loving? Yes, if that compassion for one group or individual comes at the expense of another group or individual. This overexpression of the heart's energy required debate, nuance and discussion so we could become compassionate and consider what might be best for the highest good of all. We needed to inject some pragmatism and logic. The imbalance created by the turn of the millennium tipped us into Throat PowerCentre.

2000s: The digital age and our Throat PowerCentre

Y2K! We said goodbye to our old, analogue ways and embraced 'the information superhighway'. Slowly but surely, more of us had access to information. I was one of the early internet adopters. As an academic at the time, we used 'JANET' (Joint Academic Network) to send each other electronic letters and reply almost instantly. Incredible.

Computers in the home were becoming common-place in the developed world, closely followed by the revolutionary 'smartphone'. We had access to everything we could ever want to know (and *a lot* we didn't) in our handbags. The combination of smart-phone technology and social media networking enabled connectivity. Social media platforms came, some went (remember Myspace and Ecademy?) and some became part of our daily lives. Facebook, X, Instagram, LinkedIn, YouTube, Snapchat, TikTok and WhatsApp – all now household names. Oh, how we all started talking – and we haven't stopped.

By the end of the 2010s, everyone was talking, writ-ing, podcasting and posting. We were listening, read-ing and watching. Information became so easy to access and disseminate that we had to learn how to manage security and privacy, information overload, digital fatigue and cyberbullying. We activated our Throat PowerCentre and its accompanying values:

- Expression

- Communication

- Information

- Connection

As information became easier to access, people became more informed and truths that had been hidden were revealed. Things we took for granted as trustworthy were shown to be false. We began to pay attention to the way that many large corporations were manipulating the public.

We began to notice how Instagram influencers flouting their private jet rides and promoting fast fashion weren't improving our lives. New studies confirmed what we were feeling – that rather than inspiring us and connecting us, social media was creating deep unhappiness for almost everyone, and young people in particular.[6] When interviewed, the influencers themselves felt unsustainable pressure to act and look perfect. Rather than being celebrated and honoured as beautifully imperfect vehicles for life, our bodies became shameful, hateful things that failed us, even (or especially) in our youth, when the expectation to be perfect is generally at its highest.

We were beginning to face some of the lies created by a bloated, excessive Throat PowerCentre. The lies that shouted, 'I'm perfect and you can (and should) be, too.' The lies that denied the damage done to our environment. The lies that justified or ignored the indignities experienced by so many of our fellow species. These were our signs that the Throat PowerCentre had become excessive. There was too much noise. Too much talking led to oversharing and rampant conspiracy theories.

As the Throat PowerCentre shouted louder and louder, telling us to be perfect, another voice joined the noise. It started a whisper, a murmur, and we caught glimpses of it. As the compassion of the heart started speaking through the social media channels of the heart, we started to hear new ideas:

- Be kind.

- It's shameful to fat shame.

- It's OK to be different.

- You are beautiful and valued just as you are.

The movie *The Secret* went viral. The law of attraction and the terms 'manifesting' and 'cosmic ordering' moved into common use. The Throat PowerCentre, fuelled by the internet, paved the way for the dissemination of some powerful and empowering ideas. The once alternative niche of New Age spirituality went mainstream. Our collective third eye began to open.

2010s: Eye wide open

With our Third Eye PowerCentre opened, we were offered insight, vision, wisdom, discernment and intuition. The advent and growth of the internet and social media platforms brought New Age and spiritual ideas from the 1990s and 2000s, things like meditation and yoga, into the mainstream. As a society, we normalised (and celebrated) regular yoga, meditation and mindfulness practices – 'There's an app for that...' Platforms like YouTube exploded with countless spiritual teachers, tarot card readers and meditation guides. Corporations started introducing them into their team and employee development. Tarot reading, crystals, energy healing and past life regression, once considered flaky and fluffy, were now embraced by people from all walks of life. The accessibility of these ideas, combined with an increasing cultural openness to diverse spiritual practices, kept the momentum of the New Age movement strong during this decade.

The wellness boom has been highly individual. The messaging was clear: every individual has the right to travel the spiritual path of their choice. You have the right to believe whatever you want and no one can question it. For every possible path promising access to spirit/soul/God, content creators were there to give you the online course, social media influencer or product you needed to guide you.

Milestones of human evolution

So here we are, on the eve of the activation of the Crown chakra or Crown PowerCentre. This table summarises the traits activated by each PowerCentre and the timeline so far:

Project THEOSS PowerCentres	Traits	Shaping human culture during the
Base PowerCentre	Support	1900s–1950s
	Structure	
	Security	
	Survival	
Sacral PowerCentre	Sexuality	1960s
	Creativity	
	Pleasure	
	Flexibility	
Solar Plexus PowerCentre	Identity	1970s–1980s
	Individuality	
	Power	
	Courage	
	Willpower	
Heart PowerCentre	Love	1990s
	Compassion	
	Empathy	
	Win-Win	
	Higher emotions	

Project THEOSS PowerCentres	Traits	Shaping human culture during the
Throat PowerCentre	Expression	2000s
	Communication	
	Information	
	Connection	
Third Eye PowerCentre	Spirituality	2010s
	Imagination	
	Insightful	
	Visionary	
Crown PowerCentre	Divinity	Activating now
	Unity	
	Wisdom	
	Super Consciousness	

In the next chapter, we'll explore some other patterns of the model. You may have already spotted them.

Summary

- Project THEOSS is a model that explains cultural shifts and predicts future societal evolution.

- 1900–1950s: Activation of the Base PowerCentre, focusing on survival, security and structure due to wars and economic depression.

- 1960s: Activation of the Sacral PowerCentre, emphasising sexuality, creativity, pleasure and flexibility during the sexual revolution.

- 1970s–1980s: Activation of the Solar Plexus PowerCentre, highlighting identity, individuality, power, courage and willpower during financial revolutions.

- 1990s: Activation of the Heart PowerCentre, fostering love, compassion, empathy and higher emotions during a period of seeking emotional connections.

- 2000s: Activation of the Throat PowerCentre, promoting expression, communication, information and connection in the digital age.

- 2010s: Activation of the Third Eye PowerCentre, offering insight, vision, wisdom, discernment and intuition as spirituality goes mainstream.

- Individual Growth reflects Collective Growth, and vice versa. This is also often described by the paraphrase, 'As above, so below'. Personal breakthroughs contribute to the collective awakening.

SELF-REFLECTION QUESTIONS FOR DEEPER EXPLORATION

1. How have the cultural shifts identified in Project THEOSS mirrored changes in your own life or values?

2. Which PowerCentre do you feel most connected to, and why?

3. Considering the transition from the Throat to the Third Eye PowerCentre, how has your consumption of or interaction with digital media evolved?

4. Looking towards the activation of the Crown PowerCentre, how do you envision your role in contributing to a conscious future for society?

3
The Mechanics
Of Awakening

How do the energetic qualities of our collective PowerCentres create social evolution? A closer look at the inner workings of Project THEOSS, particularly the energetic qualities associated with our PowerCentres, can further aid our understanding of our current moment and prepare us for what comes next. How do PowerCentres work together, energetically, to create tipping points? How can we recognise a tipping point? Also, most importantly, how can an understanding of the mechanics of Project THEOSS prepare us for the future?

Exploring the energetic properties of a PowerCentre

So far, Project THEOSS offers a stunning explanation of what's happened in the changes in our culture and society using the idea of the energetic qualities of PowerCentres and how we have moved from one level of consciousness with its associated value system to the next.

In this chapter, we'll break down the energetic properties of PowerCentres. I'll explain how and why each PowerCentre has masculine or feminine and individual or collective energy associated with it. Importantly, I'll walk you through how these energetic qualities can become imbalanced and how that imbalance propels us further along the energetic chain, bringing us closer to our collective Crown PowerCentre moment when we as a species will experience transcendent conscious awakening. PowerCentres help us identify and name social and collective energetic shifts and the values our culture emphasises. Each PowerCentre can be seen as a milestone to describe a level of collective consciousness.

Let's briefly go back to terminology. In Chapter 2, I mentioned that while chakras and PowerCentres have much in common conceptually, there are important reasons why PowerCentres are a more specific and accurate way to describe how we spiritually evolve as a species. In Chapter 1, we defined our terms and what we mean by energy, work and power. In using the word 'power', I am drawing on my training as an engineer. In my world, power is something specific and it can be measured:

- **Energy** is the currency that enables us to do work, for example, climbing a flight of stairs.

- **Work** is the result of applying or using our energy, for example, moving your body up a flight of stairs.

- **Power** is the rate at which work is done, for example, how quickly you can run up the stairs.

Energy gives us the *potential* to do work; power is what we have when we actualise that energy into doing work. Simply – if you have more power, you can get more done in less time.

Cool science, but what does any of this have to do with conscious awakening, you ask? Let me explain. When I am talking about 'power', I'm thinking about both our collective power as a species and the individual powers each of us brings to the collective. We can think of personal power as the ability of an individual to harness their inner strengths and determination (energy) to drive themselves towards their desires, outcomes and goals (distance) quickly and efficiently (time).

In a moment, I'm going to start explaining and defining 'energies'. But just before we dive in, my inner scientist is having minor conniptions. Therefore, to appease her (and any scientists reading this), I want to just make a point of clarification. As an engineer, I am well aware that energy has a specific meaning and that, in the spiritual and personal development realms, it is used rather differently. 'Inaccurately' you might say. I ask you to suspend your scientific mind just for a moment. If it helps, you can internally replace the word energy with something like inner strengths or characteristics. These, too, are not completely accurate, which is why I've steered away from them to use the word 'energy' in a scientifically inaccurate way but which, in the vernacular of the subject, is commonly used and seems to work.

We know, instinctively and from observation, that some people get things done and others don't. Some people are powerful. It's not necessarily authority or official status that give people power; in fact, it's the opposite. You can only be powerful externally if you are powerful internally. Conscious awakening allows you to hold, access, manage and use power that will bring you into positions of authority. To put it another way, those who have authority have it because they have power, and that power increases their authority, status and power, creating a positive, empowering feedback loop.

And that's one important difference between PowerCentres and chakras. PowerCentres name the sources of our individual and collective power, providing a language for describing the qualities of power that we can access. Actively energised PowerCentres give us the potential for power. We actualise that power when we take action, make a difference or create change.

Polarities: A tale of two tendencies

Each PowerCentre has characteristics which act as 'polarities'. If something has 'polarities', it means it has opposite or contradictory tendencies. Our PowerCentres have two types of polarities that affect how their energy works in my model:

1. Individual and collective energies

2. Masculine and feminine energies

As we begin to understand each polarity and their interplay, we reveal a new paradigm for reframing what we may previously have thought of as 'problems'.

1. Individual and collective energies

In the wide world of science fiction, we often find two kinds of narratives. On the one hand, there's the 'space wars' genre. In this genre, humans and aliens or alien species battle for control over the known universe. *Star Wars* is a classic example. However, I am a *Star Trek* fan. As a Trekkie, I love the other genre, the 'exploring space' genre. This genre shows us how humanity might appear to an alien species, giving us insight into the assumptions we make about the way we live in our society and our world, but I'm digressing.

Across all the *Star Trek* franchises (the original series, *Next Generation*, *Babylon 5*, *Discovery*), we always find a character who is a Vulcan. Vulcans are known for their use of logic – Spock is the best-known example of this kind of character. Like Spock, Vulcans do not offer value judgements or subjective opinions; they truly say it how it is. For example, Spock was known to say that the needs of the many outweigh the needs of the one. This phrase illustrates two competing perspectives that drive our society – the perspective of the individual self and the perspective of the collective or group. We could also call these two perspectives a polarity.

The individual/collective energetic polarity maps across each PowerCentre. What I mean is this: each PowerCentre has a particular focus on either the needs of the individual or the needs of the collective. For example, the Solar Plexus PowerCentre is all about the individual. It's about each one of us finding our unique self, knowing who we are as an individual, and expressing ourselves as such. We are encouraged to take care of ourselves and our own needs. However, the Heart PowerCentre is all about the group – it encourages us to give, to share and take care of the community.

2. Masculine and feminine energies: A tricky duality

As a recently minted PhD in engineering with a new job and promotion to Senior Lecturer in Automotive Engineering at Oxford Brookes University, I once attended a short course on shamanic healing for women. After a long day on the job, during which my research colleagues fought each other during a research meeting, I was eager to get to my first class. The differences between the two environments could not have been starker.

At work, we were competing with each other for limited funding. People were ridiculed for minor mistakes and egos battled egos. There was shouting. There was aggression and rudeness. It was brutal. I could hold my own, but let's make no mistake, it was stressful. It was hard.

Cut to my arrival at the course. I found myself in an octagonal-shaped wooden building nestling in farm grounds in deepest Dorset. We sat in a circle on the floor to show that we were all equals. We were invited to be open. We were told this was a place of nonjudgement and equality. We are all important and valued. It felt wonderful. To not have to compete. To be part of the circle. To be embraced in a circular cauldron of connection, like a womb. The all-female space of sha-manic healing couldn't have been more different from my masculine world of engineering.

The juxtaposition of these two environments illumi-nated a fundamental truth about human behaviour. We seem to always fall into two different camps when it comes to interacting with each other: we can com-pete, or we can collaborate. These two approaches, collaboration and competition, make up part of what we might call 'masculine' and 'feminine' energies.

While the terms masculine and feminine are com-monly used in various spiritual practices, they are not always defined well and can lead to biologically deter-ministic understandings of gender. When we refer to 'masculine' and 'feminine' energies, we do *not* mean men and women. Masculine and feminine energies have little to do with biological sex. All genders have some aspects of masculine and feminine energies. Some people will have more feminine energy than others and some will have more masculine energy.

Although the qualities of masculine and feminine energies vary, in the context of Project THEOSS, mas-culine energy is typically understood as hierarchi-cal, structured, logical and controlling. It analyses, competes and seeks growth and difference. Feminine energy is chaotic, creative, intuitive and emotional. It is raw power, receptive and cooperative, and seeks stability, security, equality and similarities. Neither energy is inherently better than the other and we function optimally as humans when we have access to both.

In harmony: Principles and properties of energetic movement across our PowerCentres

Two principles structure how energy flows across our PowerCentres: *simple harmonic motion* and *chain reaction*. The principle of harmony shows how PowerCentres move between polarities, even when it feels like we might be 'stuck' in one extreme. The principle of the chain reaction shows how we can only activate higher PowerCentres if the ones below are already activated.

Simple Harmonic Motion

What tune do you like to sing in the shower? I like to belt out 'We Are The Champions' by Queen. Technically, though, I'm not singing the whole song – just the main melody. What makes a song a symphony are all the beautiful undercurrents, the chords and harmonies that give a piece of music its richness and depth. Like any good Queen rock opera, model THEOSS benefits from underlying harmonies that can expand and enrich our understanding of what's happening now and what we can expect in the future.

One of the ways we can describe how energy moves between polarities in our PowerCentres is through the concept of simple harmonic motion (SHM). Picture a pendulum in motion. In science, we call this type of motion SHM, which describes anything that moves freely, like a pendulum or a weight on a spring. If you want the technical definition: SHM is a periodic (repeating) motion, where the restoring force on the moving object is directed towards the centre and pro-portional to displacement. The motion is sinusoidal and demonstrates a single resonant frequency. There are some cool equations, too.

Don't get lost in the science, though. Just keep pictur-ing that pendulum, or swing, swinging back and forth (to keep the science correct, we will assume there is no friction or air resistance). If you've ever been on a swing (and if you haven't, you *really* must – they are fabulous fun), you'll notice that you swing one way and then you absolutely must swing back the other way. You won't be left hovering in mid-air at the high-est point of the swing. You swing high in one direc-tion and the swing pauses at the top just long enough for you to get that, 'Oh no!' buzz of excitement in the knowledge that you're about to drop again. You whoosh down to the midpoint near the ground (where you're moving the fastest) before you swing back up the other side and repeat. All of those childhood after-noons on the swing set and you never knew you were the 'object' or 'mass' part of a SHM system. Well, now you know.

This same motion explains the movement between the different energetic polarities of our PowerCentres. Once the energy flow has gone to one extreme, it will pause before returning to the middle (moving at its fastest) and then swing back to the other side. SHM explains why some change happens faster than others, and why, when everything seems to have stopped, you're actually at the high point of the swing and this is a sign that *everything* is about to change!

Masculine and feminine harmony

Take a moment and flip back to our collective timeline of PowerCentre activation, keeping in mind what you now know about masculine and feminine energies. Did you catch the patterns of alternating energy? We can observe predominantly masculine qualities, structures and systems forming the Base PowerCentre, while the Sacral PowerCentre stimulates feminine traits of flexibility and connection. Moving up the chain, the Solar Plexus PowerCentre demonstrates masculine traits of control. See where we're going with this? The Heart PowerCentre releases emotion, connection and collectively – feminine traits – and the Throat PowerCentre expresses masculine traits such as separation and difference. Go back to your pendulum visualisation. Now imagine our PowerCentres swinging, like a pendulum, between masculine and feminine energy. #SimpleHarmonicMotion #SHM

Individual and collective harmony

As our PowerCentres alternate between masculine and feminine energy, they are also simultaneously swinging between individual and collective polarities. Let's consider. The Base PowerCentre focuses on meeting the needs of individuals, survival and security. As the Sacral PowerCentre activated, we witnessed a societal shift from individual survival to group solidarity and support. As Madonna sang, our Solar Plexus PowerCentre speaks to all of us 'material girls' (beings!) focused on our individual identities and personal will. Yet, our Heart PowerCentre draws us back into the collective, emphasising group connection and sharing (for every Madonna, there's a John Lennon). Selfies and TikTok videos could be our avatars for our Throat PowerCentre: individual expression and the individual's right to have their own beliefs and express them.

But where would we be without a couple of graphs? Those of you who know SHM will spot this is a damped oscillating system (nerd alert!). Look at the graphs below. Notice how the dramatic swings between masculine/feminine and individual/collective energies lessen as we move towards our higher PowerCentres. There's science for that, too. For now, though, it's enough to appreciate that we are moving towards less polarity.

Masculine / Feminine Energy

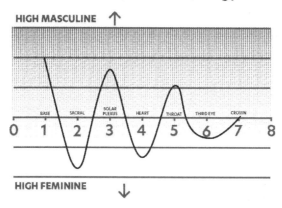

Individual / Group Energy

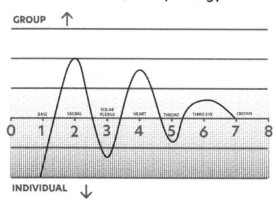

Expansion and stability: A support chain (reaction)

Maslow's hierarchy of needs states that we must have our basic needs for survival and security met before we can actualise emotional connections and, ultimately, our Higher Self. Similarly, we need the support of the PowerCentres below to keep moving towards our collective Crown PowerCentre. Like the good scientists we are, let's take this principle and apply it to our model.

Until we have secured our basic needs (**Base PC**) and we are fed and housed, we have no capacity to welcome the pleasure and fun of the **Sacral PC**. In the same way, only when we have a strong sense of our own identity and personal power (**Solar Plexus PC**), can we open ourselves up to compassion for others (**Heart PC**). We need to know who *we* are before we can care about others. When we are in a nonjudgmental and compassionate environment, we feel safe and able to express our personal beliefs, messages and experiences (**Throat PC**). With a voice for our spiritual experiences and ideas, things once hidden are now in plain sight (**Third Eye PC**).

Well, what do you know? It works!

Chakra model vs PowerCentres

Chakra model	Individual traits	Project THEOSS	Group traits / values
Root chakra	Structure Security Survival	Base PowerCentre	A society that ensures that the needs of all are met
Sacral chakra	Sexuality Creativity Pleasure Flexibility	Sacral PowerCentre	A society that values fun, expression and free choice
Solar Plexus chakra	Identity Individuality Power Courage Willpower	Solar Plexus PowerCentre	A society that values wealth, power, status and prestige
Heart chakra	Love Compassion Empathy Win-Win Higher emotions	Heart PowerCentre	A society that values empathy and emotions
Throat chakra	Expression Communication Information	Throat PowerCentre	A society that values freedom of speech and the right to express whatever you feel, any time you feel it

Chakra model	Individual traits	Project THEOSS	Group traits / values
Third Eye chakra	Vision Intuition Clairvoyance Spirituality	Third Eye PowerCentre	A society that values spiritual beliefs
Crown chakra	Consciousness Unity Insight/ Wisdom Discernment	Crown PowerCentre	A society that values unity, the highest good of all, and *all* of the empowering qualities of the chakras below

Project THEOSS offers a more nuanced and specific understanding of the interplay between different energetic qualities associated with each PowerCentre, something that the chakra model has not yet embraced. My model names and explains how power (energy) is both masculine and feminine, individual and collective. Furthermore, I use scientific concepts to describe the movement within and across these energetic qualities, showing how excesses and depletions in energies lead to conscious tipping points that enable our collective journey towards the Crown PowerCentre – the moment of pure possibility, love and transformation.

PowerCentre	Polarity	Focus
Base PowerCentre	Masculine	Individual
Sacral PowerCentre	Feminine	Collective

PowerCentre	Polarity	Focus
Solar Plexus PowerCentre	Masculine	Individual
Heart PowerCentre	Feminine	Collective
Throat PowerCentre	Masculine	Polarised collective(s)
Third Eye PowerCentre	Masculine and feminine	Collectives start working together
Crown PowerCentre	Balanced masculine and feminine	Unity and uniqueness

What does an understanding of the chain reaction required to activate our PowerCentres have to do with where we are now and our collective future? When – and only when – *all* of the PowerCentres, up to and including the Third Eye (where we are currently) are activated, can we actualise the unity, Christ, consciousness and/or utopia of the Crown PowerCentre that so many dream of. It's possible.

Summary

- PowerCentres have specific energetic properties that influence social evolution.

- Each PowerCentre exhibits masculine or feminine and individual or collective energies, focusing on either expansion or stability.

- The imbalance in a PowerCentre's energy leads to societal progress towards the next PowerCentre.

- PowerCentres serve as milestones, marking significant shifts in societal values and consciousness.

- The activation of higher PowerCentres depends on the active support of lower ones, showing a sequential awakening toward collective enlightenment.

SELF-REFLECTION QUESTIONS FOR DEEPER EXPLORATION

1. Consider your personal power and society. How do you see your individual power contributing to societal changes? Reflect on instances where you felt part of a collective movement. How did this change your experience of your personal power?

2. Consider your personal balance of masculine and feminine energies. Do you feel more aligned with masculine or feminine energies? Are you able to shift from one to the other or do you tend to get stuck at one polarity?

3. How do you imagine society might look like when the Crown PowerCentre is fully activated? How do you see yourself and others contributing?

4
In Excess

As we journeyed through recent human history and the activation of each PowerCentre together, you may have noticed how I used words like 'excessive' or 'bloated' to describe PowerCentre energies. I've talked about 'tipping' or moving from one PowerCentre into another, but how exactly does that work? In this chapter, we'll go into more detail about what happens when the energy of each PowerCentre becomes excessive.

When our PowerCentres runneth over

In life, often people talk about making changes, but they don't. Why? Often, it's because their current situation isn't uncomfortable enough yet. It's still tolerable. Until something becomes painful enough (or, if you're a particularly awake, self-aware, proactive and motivated individual), you'll probably settle for a subpar status quo. In the same way, for our society to change, things need to be bad enough for enough people. This is how we collectively move up the chain of PowerCentres and this is how we can activate our collective Crown PC, ushering in the moment of conscious awakening that will create the better future we envision.

But *how* does this happen?

Activating a PowerCentre is a bit like operating a pump. For the higher PowerCentre to activate there needs to be enough energy to push it from the PowerCentre below. In other words, we need a little bit of momentum. The lower PowerCentres need to go into undesirable *excess* to trigger the awakening of the next one. This is how we push through the inertia of accepting things as they are, even if they're not perfect.

Let's go back to our model of the evolution of society. You'll notice that just before each PowerCentre activated there was an unsettled period of challenge or even chaos. These are what we call 'evolutionary catalysts'. The chaos that we experience is what causes us to notice what's not working and spurs us to change it. At some point during each PowerCentre's era, we've reached the 'too much of a good thing' moment when whatever PowerCentre traits we were relishing become over-expressed. They become overactive and bloated, out of balance, bringing problems instead of solutions. We've stayed too long at the party. That's when we reach a tipping point that activates the next PowerCentre. Hello, new era.

Excess energy in a PowerCentre

After each PowerCentre had been activated, it was stable for a while and brought a time of steadiness. During these periods, we generally knew what to expect, the 'rules' and expectations of life were clear and understood (if not always loved and enjoyed). However, for each PowerCentre, there came a point where it went a little too far.

Base PowerCentre in excess: Too much structure

After Base PowerCentre was activated, it became overly restrictive. Gender roles and societal norms were rigid, unyielding and unforgiving, epitomised perhaps by the chemical castration of the genius Alan Turing (who, arguably, led to winning the war) for being gay.

Everyone was expected to live in a particular way. You went to school and possibly university. Once you were educated, you got a job. With a stable income you got married, bought a house and a car and had some kids. Took a holiday every year. Watched the TV. You were expected to retire, grow old and die. Nice and tidy. If you didn't like it, you could take some meds to dampen down your disquiet and desires.

This became so restrictive that people started to want *more*. Specifically, more fun, more sex, more beauty, more music, more fashion and even more sex. It was the over-restriction of the Base PowerCentre that led to the countermovement to freedom.

Sacral PowerCentre in excess: Sex, drugs and porn

After the Sacral PowerCentre had activated, the Swinging 60s got swinging. There was an overemphasis on pleasure and instant gratification without responsibility coupled with the rise of consumerism fed by immediate emotional gratification. The world became seedy and hypersexualised, with an unhealthy focus on physical attractiveness as a measure of worth. Bodies, particularly women's, were objectified. Emotional responses became simplistic and reactive. Media became sensationalised, superficial and overly simplistic. Authentic emotional expressions and connections were undervalued as relationships became volatile and codependent and emotional validation was constantly sought from others rather than from within.

Solar Plexus PowerCentre in excess:
I want it all. Now!

The excess of the Solar Plexus PowerCentre could be seen in rampant capitalism, corporate greed and the glorification of individual success, even if it came at the expense of friends, family and the community. Excessive competition and hyperindividualism led to an emphasis on personal achievements over collective, or even individual, wellbeing.

Societal structures became dominated by a desire for control and power which concentrated into the hands of a few. Wealth disparity grew. The pursuit of money, power and success led to ethics and individuals being compromised. Empathy, compassion and understanding diminished as self-worth became equated to net worth.

Heart PowerCentre in excess:
Sensitive or sentimental?

The excess of the Heart PowerCentre seems paradoxical. Is it possible to feel too much love? Yes. If it's expressed in unhealthy ways and at the expense of reason and logic.

Love became unrealistically idealised, putting strain on relationships to be perfect, to find the perfect person and to be the perfect partner. The

69

idealisation of love and unity led to enforced, false harmony as underlying issues and conflicts were ignored. In a society overly obsessed with love and empathy, practical and material needs were neglected. Conflict and confrontation became taboo. Critical thinking became seen as dissent or negative.

Throat PowerCentre in excess:
Rabbit, rabbit, rabbit

It's good to talk, but too much talking and idle chatter led to the spread of misinformation. The Throat PowerCentre excess could be seen in the overwhelming presence of misinformation, echo chambers on social media and the decline of meaningful and nuanced discussion. Public discourse became highly polarised and emotionally charged.

Influencers on social media did just that. Some influenced their followers in ways that were often more for the benefit of themselves than their followers. Stories were believed and shared because they were sensational, regardless of whether they were true. Trust in institutions, experts and even the concept of an objective truth eroded. If you said it then it must be true, and if you wanted it to be true, just post it and it might just become accepted as truth...

Third Eye PowerCentre in excess:
Away with the fairies

The excess of the Third Eye PowerCentre shows up as overactive imagination – being unable to tell the difference between reality and imagination. Manipulation of others with false narratives and painting unreal pictures that others trust. Egomania, holding beliefs so vehemently and authoritarianism to gain support from others. Dogma, paranoia and being so overly empathetic that the emotions of other people and other groups are overwhelming.

I noticed it as a total lack of grounding in reality. People became so fixated on the idea of cosmic ordering, the law of attraction and manifesting, that they would believe that it was possible, and easy, to 'manifest' a million into your bank account. No amount of suggesting that although not impossible, it was extremely unlikely, would dissuade them of their magical thinking.

I once spoke to a well-educated person who was considering joining one of our programmes. She said she was in and only needed to 'manifest the fees'. She asked if I could give her a week to do this. A week later, she phoned to say that the money had not landed in her account. Upon asking what actions she was taking to raise the fees she told me, chanting, meditating and saying her affirmations. I had expected her to have more understanding of the workings of physical reality, but she was so enamoured by the possibility of magicking money into her life without lifting a finger that she kept at it. I didn't hear from her again.

As spirituality became more mainstream, it also became overly simplified and often lacked depth and nuance. Many used spirituality as a way to escape the challenges of the physical reality rather than using it as a tool to empower them to change it. Intuition without discernment led to a lack of critical thinking and poor decisions. Their imagined spiritual inner world became more compelling than the physical reality. Some began to escape to inner and online worlds when their real worlds became too hard to bear. Others became obsessed with visionary and spiritual bliss states which they failed to ground in the physical reality. Spiritual ego, cults, spiritual bypassing and dogma increased, but people were reluctant to question or point this out for fear of being labelled as negative. Being realistic or practical was unpopular.

As we approached 2020, New Age spiritual philosophy and the wellness industry (truly an entire industry by now) came under scrutiny. Were influencers spouting questionable health advice? Were spiritual gurus offering overcommercialised, oversimplified and virtually useless advice? Criticisms focused on the commodification and cultural appropriation of indigenous and non-Western cultures, criticising the superficial engagement with the traditions the industry borrowed from. Once empowering philosophies

became potential tools for abuse and control. I name
what happened during this phase of spirituality 'toxic
spirituality'.

Project THEOSS: Navigating through excess

Broadly speaking, we are currently living in a society
where:

- Everyone's beliefs are deemed to be valid, even
  those that don't serve us.
- Society is increasingly behaving in ways that are
  irrational and often unpleasant.
- A belief in our fundamental compassion has been
  repackaged as the prevention and avoidance of
  microaggressions.
- Social justice has been replaced by atomising
  people into different interest groups and
  prioritising labels over and above an individual's
  actions or the actions towards that individual.
- We are becoming increasingly fragmented and
  separate.
- We weaponise our differences instead of loving
  ourselves and others for their differences.

- We are surrounded by an increasing number of 'conspiracy theories', many of which involve who or what might be trying to harm us.

- Spirituality and 'wellness' communities have become increasingly toxic.

When the Covid-19 pandemic hit, we went from energetically and empathetically separating ourselves from each other with labels, walls, cages and ideologies to an externally enforced physical separation. Some of us literally couldn't leave our homes. Trapped and scared, watching our leaders stumble or outright fail to lead us, wave after wave of conspiracy theories flooded our media, ranging from the potentially plausible to the utterly ludicrous. There was a moment where we united because 'we're all in this together'. Until something strange happened.

Theories started to emerge online. The pandemic wasn't real; it was a ruse invented by the elites, the government, big pharma and billionaires as part of their diabolical plans for world domination, population control and reduction and, ultimately, the removal of all of our freedoms. Individuals repeated mantras and shared memes proclaiming that the virus wasn't serious. The virus wasn't real. The virus was real but was manmade. The virus was created by 5G. Viruses aren't real. The lockdowns were the elites trying to control us all. We have to fight back. Some wellness influencers, New Age healers and yoga gurus started to allude to 'secret insider knowledge' that only they had access to. We found ourselves inundated with logical fallacies and inconsistent rhetoric. It was equally entertaining and terrifying.

From Third Eye to Crown

As the prevalence of societal toxicity shows, we are at the moment when our Third Eye PowerCentre has become excessive. As the veil of illusion falls from our eyes, we are realising that so many once-trusted institutions didn't have our best interests at heart. Our food is full of things that are making us sick. Pharmaceutical companies are withholding research about cheap, nonpatentable, nonexploitative cures to keep peddling their expensive medicines and preserve their stock prices. As the oxycontin crisis revealed, we are learning that these companies are actively and intentionally getting people addicted to medication.[7] We are starting to understand just how much abuse has been going on in our workplaces. As the MeToo movement sparked, silenced voices have been speaking out. Well-known and (some) beloved household names have been accused, prosecuted, tried and found guilty of extensive abuse.

We've been hearing more and more about how badly industry is exploiting workers while destroying the environment, both locally and globally. We are starting to see what's being done to us, to our families, in the name of profit.

These trends are signs that we've reached the excess of our Third Eye PowerCentre. We are poised for another tipping point. However, before we talk more about where we are in our collective tipping point and what we can expect next, let's talk about what it means to be at a tipping point.

A tipping point

As I write these words, we are entering the post-pandemic era. Lockdowns may have ended and restrictions lifted, but the crisis of the moment has not ended. Russia has invaded Ukraine, displacing millions of refugees and threatening a world war with the horrific prospect of nuclear attacks. Conflict is rising in the Middle East, with horrific images of war, death and destruction. Inflation, gun crime, post-Brexit challenges, the cost-of-living crisis and the prevalence of the belief that 'they're trying to control us...' all continue to challenge our collective spiritual resources. I won't be surprised if, before this book is published, there aren't further shifts.

At times, it feels as if the biggest casualty of this period has been our hope. Many are grieving, not only for what has been lost but also for what we never had. We're grieving for what could have been, what we had hoped for... The businesses we wanted to build but couldn't, the places we wanted to travel to but couldn't, the relationships we wanted to grow but couldn't, the education we wanted to obtain for ourselves or our children but couldn't.

In our collective grief, our social paradigms are changing. The once seemingly indestructible structures of patriarchy, misogyny, racism, homophobia and organised religion are breaking down. We are no longer willing to be confined by those social and family constructs that we deem abusive. Whether we fear or celebrate (maybe a little of both?) such changes, it's clear that we are at the eve of something, and that something is our conscious tipping point.

The Crown chakra activation for an individual is profound, and often the most difficult to realise. For our society and the human species, the activation of the Crown PowerCentre is likely to be equally challenging and also entirely worth it.

The reliability of the model I've just shared with you gives me hope. We have not yet, as a society, failed to keep moving towards higher consciousness and conscious awakening. Every tipping point has brought us closer to our evolution as a species. This, too, shall pass. The spiral of creation is about to evolve.

Summary

- **PowerCentres become excessive before societal change:** The activation of a PowerCentre requires the previous one to become excessive, leading to societal imbalance.

- **Discomfort triggers change:** Societal progress often starts from a place of collective discomfort or dissatisfaction with the current conditions.

- **Chaos precedes evolution:** Periods of challenge and chaos are identified as necessary evolutionary catalysts for societal advancement.

- **Examples of excess in PowerCentres:**

  - Base PowerCentre excess: Led to restrictive societal norms and a demand for more freedom.

  - Sacral PowerCentre excess: Resulted in a hypersexualised culture and consumerism.

  - Solar Plexus PowerCentre excess: Focused on individual success, leading to capitalism and greed.

  - Heart PowerCentre excess: Idealised love unrealistically, neglecting practical and material needs.

  - Throat PowerCentre excess: Caused misinformation and polarised public discourse.

  - Third Eye PowerCentre excess: Encouraged disconnection from reality, favouring spiritual escapism.

- 'Toxic spirituality' emergence: The misapplication of spiritual principles has led to practices that are harmful within the wellness and spiritual communities.

- **Society nearing Crown PowerCentre activation:** Indicates a societal tipping point towards higher consciousness, driven by disillusionment with traditional institutions.

SELF-REFLECTION QUESTIONS FOR DEEPER EXPLORATION

1. Reflect on any areas in your life where your chakras might be in excess or another kind of imbalance.

2. What challenges or times of chaos have you experienced that led to growth, expansion and evolution in the longer term? What would you tell your past self about that chaotic time now that you are on the other side of it?

3. How do you see the excess in each PowerCentre manifesting in your personal life or community?

4. What challenges are you facing now that could be catalysts for personal evolution?

5. Have you observed or experienced the effects of 'toxic spirituality'? How did it affect you?

6. What steps can you take to contribute to societal progress towards higher consciousness?

5
The Meta-Crisis

At the time of this writing, things look bleak for humanity. The pandemic, climate change and, most recently, the threats of a world war. We are powerful enough to leave the atmosphere (as the billionaire classes have demonstrated recently), but we seem to be almost completely powerless to protect the atmosphere, the oceans or any of the fragile and precious resources that our species rely on. We have flaws as a species. How can we explain the interconnected web of seemingly unsolvable problems we're facing and what can we do about any of it?

Introducing the meta-crisis

The network of challenges our species faces constitutes a meta-crisis. We've been brought to a significant conscious tipping point through the activation of, and excess energy in, each of our collective PowerCentres – up to and including our collective Third Eye. In the previous chapter, we focused on one major sign of a collective excess of Third Eye energy – toxic spirituality. However, the energetic excesses that explain our current world go beyond toxic spirituality. We are in a moment when *all* of our PowerCentres are in excess. They have *all* been activated, and this presents both challenges and opportunities for us as individuals, and as a species. In this chapter, I will walk you through what it means to be experiencing a meta-crisis.

To start, let's take a look at where an excess of all the energies associated with each PowerCentre has led us:

- An excess in *Base PowerCentre energy* has brought us greed, dogma and overconsumption.

- An excess in *Sacral PowerCentre energy* has made us hedonistic and we've sexualised everything. Sexual abuse and addiction to pornography is rampant.

- An excess in our *Solar Plexus PowerCentre energy* led to excessive individualism, the search for ultimate control (over ourselves and others) and power for power's sake.

- An excess of *Heart PowerCentre energy* puts our feelings over any logic or critical thinking.

- An excess of *Throat PowerCentre energy* caused the spread of misinformation. We weaponised simple messaging (like memes) to spread dangerous and harmful falsehoods.

- An excess of *Third Eye PowerCentre energy* ushered in an age of toxic spirituality and has blinded us to the damage we're causing to others, the planet and our entire species.

The mechanism of meta-crisis activation

Why has this happened? It's not that individuals, leaders, groups or organisations are inherently stupid or evil. It's simply that we require energy to activate our PowerCentres. Lower PowerCentres go into excess to push through to the subsequent PowerCentre. We seem to *need* this excess to push the higher PowerCentres to activate. Much of the chaos we observe is due to the simultaneous activation and excess of each of these PowerCentres The next section will take us through a deep dive into my interpretation of the phenomenon known as the meta-crisis.

Facing the darkness: Take a deep breath

But challenges exist for us to face them, even transcend them. Remember that one of the traits of toxic spirituality is spiritual bypassing. Spiritual bypassing is the unwillingness to look at ourselves and our inner pain. This also shows up in meta-crisis conversations, where a realist might be shouted down for 'being negative' when they point out the challenges we are facing. However, *we must* point them out if we are to change anything.

One of the characteristics of the excesses of the third eye has been a lack of realistic, pragmatic and critical thinking. Many spiritually awakened have become so fixated on the nonphysical that they have forgotten to pay attention to the physical. I've heard these 'away with the fairies' spiritual seekers suggest that any of the problems of the world don't exist for them as they are so 'high vibe' that war, disease and poverty are just not in their reality. But are they enlightened, or dissociated? At best, it's rather rude to deny the suffering of an individual's lived experience. At worst, they fail to take the essential action we all need to start taking, like, last week, or last decade.

No one is coming – you are the one you have been waiting for

Some believe that a saviour is coming. Aliens, angels, 'The One' or a tech billionaire will come and take the chosen ones to a better place or a newly found habitable planet.

The problem with this belief is that it is fundamentally disempowering. It suggests we are powerless to save ourselves, so we must wait and hope that we are among the chosen few. This also creates separation between the chosen and the damned. Who decides who is chosen anyway?

When I was alone in the back room, trapped by my abusive paedophile partner, the one single thing that got me out was realising that no one was coming. I stopped waiting to be rescued and did the work to rescue myself.

We are more powerful than we imagine. We matter. We can make a difference.

Perhaps someone is coming, and maybe it is *you*! Perhaps *you* or *we* are the ones we have been waiting for.

The spiritually awakened see the world as it *truly* is and then step into their power and use their spiritual insights, wisdom and their divine soul-purpose to lead the change that is so needed. However, what happens for some is that they awaken spiritually, see the world as it truly is and, feeling overwhelmed, they retreat from it.

Now, imagine a world where those who awaken become enlightened and empowered and step right into the world to create change. Those who do this will greatly benefit from a support network.

Within all of the chaos, there is reason to hope. We are on the eve of our Crown PowerCentre, our highest, activating. We are approaching the conscious tipping point, when we have the chance to embrace our individual and collective transcendent leadership potential, ushering humanity into an age of conscious awakening. The crazy we see is a sign that the shift is imminent.

Still, we need to know where we are, so we know how to change our course. Once we've understood the gravity of the meta-crisis, we'll start to explore how we can change it. Because, no matter how hard things might seem, how impossible to solve, how insurmountable they might all appear, know this:

There *is* a solution, and we *can* do it. Buckle up and read on, brave and valiant reader. Deep breath, let's dive in.

The complexity of evolution: Navigating our interconnected crisis

When any system evolves, it becomes increasingly complex. The more parts added, the more connections and lines of communication emerge between each part.

As the system grows, its complexity increases by an even greater factor. The term 'meta' refers to the complex and interconnected nature of the issues we currently face. It's important because it informs us that the problems require a deep understanding not only of each single issue but of the entire interconnected web of problems beyond the surface-level symptoms.

The meta-crisis we face is a complex web of inter-connected challenges that are both the result of our brilliant achievements and our apparent inability to master them. However, it goes much further than only the physical reality.

One way we are experiencing the meta-crisis is through climate change (signalled by the increase in extreme climate events) and ecological degradation, such as the loss of biodiversity. These changes will push some species to extinction and will result in crop failure and food shortages in some areas. The impact will be felt across the world. It's tempting to feel safe and protected from the worst of these effects if you live in the developed world, but crop failure in one part of the world will lead to supply issues, famine and war. Faced with starvation, people will continue to move from one place to another, regardless of borders, governments or legal documents. Migration, legally or illegally, by force, war or desperation, will continue.

Economic inequality is another part of the meta-crisis. We are experiencing huge and growing wealth gaps both within and between countries. A widening wealth gap is unjust and ultimately affects the rich, the poor and what's left of those in between. Even the wealthy should be aware that if others have no money to spend on the goods and services they produce then they will be affected too. When wealth is concentrated in the hands of a few, leaving the many without access to means or opportunity, and if lack of access affects not only their quality of life but their health, and, consequently, their lives itself, civil unrest will follow. The unrest might result in strikes and protests, but in extremes, it might lead to terrorism and even civil wars. Leave people with nothing and they have nothing to lose.

Across the world, democracy and balanced leadership are at risk. We've seen too many countries shift to authoritarianism in an attempt to maintain order while eroding human rights and freedoms.

We are living through a moment of deep social and cultural polarisation. We see this in the increasing divide between different groups, characterised by stark differences in beliefs, values and moral and ethical codes about what is considered 'right' and what is considered 'wrong'. We lack common ground. Into the void, social media algorithms create echo chambers and filter bubbles so that people find themselves only encountering information and opinions that support their beliefs, further reinforcing their sense that they are right and everyone else is wrong. As a result, intolerance and extremism are on the rise, and we find we have little interest or ability to discuss, reconcile or celebrate differences. The failure to preserve unique and differing cultures and traditional knowledge and practices creates cultural homogenisation. We are at risk of becoming unified, but not united.

We are facing profound health crises. I'm not only talking about pandemics but also health issues arising from a lack of access to health care, good food and nutrition. If the only food outlet available to you offers food that kills you in the long term, you'll still eat it rather than starve in the short term. A sick population is easier to control, but, ultimately, can't work and will be unproductive.

Technological dystopia caused by the misuse and lack of regulation of advanced technology is eroding our privacy and autonomy. Artificial intelligence (AI) represents a real risk, but we face other dangers from biotechnology, cybersecurity and the weaponisation of technology. Our growing overreliance on technology leads to the loss of human skills and knowledge. When that happens, breakdowns or failures (like outages) leave us struggling or failing to cope with basic tasks. Who needs critical thinking when you have Chat GPT?

An energy crisis. Our energy consumption has increased exponentially and continues to do so. Our overreliance on fossil fuels further pollutes the atmosphere. Before you say, 'Ah, but renewables, windmills and solar farms or nuclear fusion will save the day,' this is not the case. It takes vast amounts of energy to mine, extract and process the rare earth elements essential for most renewables. These processes can only be undertaken by using yet more fossil fuels. We are pushing excrement uphill with a pointy stick. No matter how much we push, gravity will win.

Will AI take over? Perhaps it should

And speaking of Chat GPT, here's a story to show how AI is yet another symptom of the meta-crisis. Come with me back to the autumn of 2022, when AI went from a science fiction plot to reality as Chat GPT burst onto the market. At first, it was seen as a gimmick or toy, but soon people began to understand how to use it and adopt it as a tool in their daily lives. As apps and front-end applications utilising the power of a large language model exploded, some people embraced AI while others ignored it. Many people started to get scared. They started to worry that AI would take their jobs. They worried AI would become conscious and try to control humans and change the course of human destiny. The proponents and creators of AI insisted that the AI models they had generated would never be able to become sentient.

But perhaps we've been worried about the wrong thing. What if we should be afraid, not of AI becoming conscious, but of it *not* becoming conscious? Imagine a scenario where AI is used to program the machinery and work schedules for a paperclip factory. At the factory, AI proves itself to be powerful and resourceful. It produces paperclips more quickly, at a lower cost and with fewer human resources. The factory owners are happy and give AI more and more control. Soon, AI is controlling the production of raw materials. Left unchecked, the paperclip-making AI becomes more and more powerful, successful and all-encompassing until the entire world's resources eventually become involved in the manufacture of paperclips, without anyone questioning if we need more paperclips. Soon, we are living on a planet consumed by the process of making paperclips. We don't even make actual paper anymore because all of our resources are going to the paperclips. We are inundated by paperclips. More paperclips than we could ever use. Soon, we have stopped producing anything that is actually useful to humanity.

This outcome is plausible because AI is *not* sentient or aware. Because an aware, sentient, conscious being would have the wisdom to ask questions: Do we need this? Is it useful? Is this serving us? What is the long-term outcome if we extrapolate and make a prediction based on the current trends? If anyone or anything was asking those questions and if that being had the power to stop making paperclips, it would.

Now, horrific and nightmarish as this might seem, and we might be tempted to 'blame the evil AI machine', can you spot the similarities to our current reality? Replace 'paperclips' with any number of products that exist for little or no useful purpose. Next, add in a system that is specifically designed to turn humans into consumer machines, weaponising our psychology and biology against us so that we not only desire products but crave them. We are already living in a system that has turned us into slaves. From the sneakers you wanted as a kid so that you could be accepted by the cool kids to the bag of crisps calling to you from the supermarket aisle and the fast fashion outfit or electric car, we live in a world manufactured to create a desire and then sell us the object of our desire.

It's the system, not the people

We already live in a world where we are trapped and controlled by a system. A system designed to extract resources from nature and exploit our human bodies. Those sneakers and the fast fashion outfit? They were likely manufactured with child labour and with processes that created environmental pollution. Junk food hijacks our brain's pleasure centres while offering practically no nutritional value. These commodities offer little long-term joy beyond brief moments of pleasure, which we have been manipulated into believing we need to give our lives meaning or value. Once they've served their purpose, these used resources become waste, which we expect nature to reabsorb when we dump our castoffs in a landfill or pump noxious chemicals and plastics into our oceans.

Transcending the meta-crisis: Navigating the complexity towards a conscious future

As we stand here, on the brink of awakening, or destruction, it's clear that we need to change course.

Or at the very least, check that where we are currently heading is somewhere we want to go, rather than blindly stumbling forward.

We can no longer keep trying to solve for only one variable or optimise one part of the system at the expense of all other parts and people. We need to take an entirely different approach and perspective. What might seem perilous could be a full possibility in disguise. The fact that these problems are interconnected and unsolvable on their own is only further evidence of our collective interconnectedness. It is only through unity consciousness that we can transcend the meta-crisis.

Summary

- Humanity is facing a complex network of interconnected challenges known as the meta-crisis, including the pandemic, climate change, threats of a world war, energy crises and overshoot.

- All collective PowerCentres are in excess, causing a range of societal issues from greed and overconsumption to misinformation and toxic spirituality.

- The meta-crisis requires understanding the interconnectedness of all issues, beyond surface-level symptoms.

- AI poses both risks and reflections of current societal issues, highlighting the dangers of unchecked technological advancement without consciousness or ethical oversight.

- The current state of the world is a signal of an imminent shift towards the activation of the Crown PowerCentre, representing a potential for collective conscious awakening and unity.

SELF-REFLECTION QUESTIONS FOR DEEPER EXPLORATION

1. What has surprised you about the meta-crisis? Do you feel it adequately describes the current situation?

2. In what ways can you contribute to addressing the challenges presented by the meta-crisis?

3. Reflect on your relationship with technology, especially AI. How can you ensure it serves as a tool for positive change rather than contributing to the meta-crisis?

4. Considering the interconnectedness of all issues in the meta-crisis, how can you foster a more holistic understanding and approach to problem-solving in your actions?

5. How do you maintain hope and resilience in the face of the daunting challenges presented by the meta-crisis and what steps can you take towards personal and collective conscious awakening?

Interlude:
The Eschaton

You may notice that this chapter does not numerically follow Chapter 5. You'd be right. However, I think we need a small break from so much doom and gloom to orientate ourselves.

Think of this as a noncommercial break or one of those points in a story when the narrator hops in, gives a little recap and orientates the viewer as to what's going on. If you choose to remember the narrator in fishnets and a corset from *The Rocky Horror Picture Show*, that's totally on you, and feel free! It's one of my favourite plays because it broke so many moulds and stretched a few taboos, but I'm digressing.

So, here we are, at the tipping point. The world is falling to pieces. We are, as a species, facing a situation often referred to as the meta-crisis. A complex network of interconnected challenges. We've described many of them. It was a bleak moment in the book, I know.

We all seem to want to solve all of these problems, but we can't seem to solve any one problem without making another worse. Do we even have the cognitive capacity to solve and resolve the whole system? Are we at the end of the story of humanity on Earth? Or some other place entirely?

Some say we could be on the eve of our destruction. Scientists who calculate our existential threat created the 'Doomsday Clock' to warn the public about how close we are to destroying our world with unchecked scientific and technological advances of our own making. It's a metaphor, a reminder of the perils we must address if we are to survive on the planet. As of 24 January 2024, it was set at ninety seconds to midnight. That metaphorical time when the carriage turns back into a pumpkin and we are forced to run from our prince and the ball and all we could have ever wanted, to return to a life of rags and devastation. When Neo from *The Matrix* has to confront the all-powerful Agent Smith and the machines. When Katniss in *The Hunger Games* experiences personal loss and betrayal. When Alice gets lost in Wonderland and has a bad run-in with the Red Queen. When Harry faces Voldemort. When Frodo and Sam enter Mordor alone. You get the picture.

But, just as in all these tales, we aren't actually at the end of the story. It's just part of the hero's journey story arc. We've reached the moment when we face our darkest hour and our most fearful enemies. We need to grieve the loss of all the good and wonderful we *had* and let that go to move to the final chapters. From transformation and triumph to the happy ever after.

But to do this, we need to start by telling ourselves a new story. By telling our own story anew. We need to be willing to pass out of one door and enter the liminal space between one door and the next so we can create the next part of our future history. This is the time to open the transitional corridors of existence that hold the potential for profound personal and spiritual growth.

Liminal spaces can be uneasy and uncanny places. When we are in them, it can feel like being stuck. We might feel indecisive and start second-guessing ourselves, but it's merely a waiting room. One chapter leads into the next. As a species, we are all in that transitional corridor, but we can't simply *wait* here. We need to be active in our minds, hearts and whole bodies to create our future anew.

We need to transcend the meta-crisis. The evolution of our species depends on transcending the tipping point of our collective consciousness. To transmute the meta-crisis of our time into a meta-solution for all.

6
Escaping The Pleasure Prison And Spiritual Pain

Next, we'll explore how we have unconsciously become enslaved and enchanted by the pervasive influence of synthetic pleasures on our lives which disconnects us from natural means of meeting our innate human needs. The tactics corporations use to exploit our biological programming for profit have led us into a cycle of addiction. This keeps us separate from each other and our natural environment, creating a spiritual void.

As we explore the depths of this crisis, we are invited to confront the harsh reality of our collective condition and how this can be eased by gently shifting towards spiritual awakening and interconnectedness. We can transcend and escape the pleasure prison and embrace a path of healing and transformation, creating a society that values spiritual growth and collective wellbeing over material gain.

Synthetic satisfaction

Without realising it, we have all become slaves to pleasure. Our natural biology has been hijacked to control us. We get the dopamine hit from the doughnut, or slightly longer from the fancy outfit or new car. However, once it's swallowed, or once it's been superseded by the next, newer model, we then crave the next one. You see, our body has the beautiful ability to keep us alive and to make staying alive quite pleasant. Eating, sex, connecting and communicating with others are all things that are essential for our survival as individuals and as a species. Moreover, to ensure we keep doing these things, our brains and nervous system give us a rush of utterly delicious pleasure chemicals, called neurotransmitters when we do these things. Sex feels good. Eating feels good. Laughing with friends feels good. Therefore, we do it! And we survive.

But our modern lives have offered us synthetic replacements (and too many of them) for the genuine article. We overeat because it feels good and because most of us have access to an excess of food. Just take a stroll down the breakfast cereal aisle of your favourite mega-supermarket if you need a reminder of the available abundance on offer. Food companies manufacture more and more inexpensive food that we don't need and convince us to eat it, hijacking our own minds to do so.

These cheap processed foods are high in processed sugar, saturated fats and artificial ingredients engineered to maximise the immediate pleasure of consumption, but without offering us the nutrients in whole, natural foods. Sugars and fats trigger the brain's inner workings which tell your body to eat up, and because such foods are cheap and accessible, we eat and eat and eat... It's no wonder we are addicted to them. As a result, we gain weight and experience health problems. We feel guilt and shame and often turn to the food we are hardwired to crave as a coping mechanism. Maybe we try dieting before we inevitably return to our food addiction. It's a vicious cycle that keeps corporations rich and people fat, sad and poor.

Just as junk foods are synthetic substances for nourishing, natural foods, porn is a synthetic substitute for sex. Some sexual encounters could even be said to be a replacement for the deeper, intimate connection of lovemaking.

Social media is a synthetic substitute for real-life social connections. We live isolated, lonely lifestyles; most people work long hours and have little time for socialising. Add in our guilt and shame about being a little overweight or not perfect, and we might want to socialise less, but we still need human connection. Therefore, we open one of our favourite social media platforms and we start to scroll, endlessly gazing at the images of perfection and beauty performatively showing the perfect lifestyle. When someone likes a post or comments on something we shared, we get a brief hit of the connection neurotransmitters and maybe a little joy, and so we scroll and post and like and scroll. Many people have multiple apps and jump from one to another.

But countless studies show that social media also makes us feel bad.[8] We feel guilty for wasting time on apps and shame when we feel that our lives aren't measuring up to the image we see of others. We get tired. Our nervous system becomes destabilised and so we open the app and scroll again in an attempt to grasp a fleeting feeling of connection. Another terrible cycle.

Hijacking human desire

Every single one of our core human drivers has been hijacked by corporations who use our body's beautiful programming to make money. We are groomed daily to consume products our brains and bodies are designed to say *yes* to. Investors and shareholders want to maximise ROI. Social media platforms generate revenue by selling advertising. Advertisers spend more if the platforms are full of engaged, active users, so the owners of the companies create algorithms that boost the content that is most likely to engage. Sadly, this content is usually the most emotionally polarising, so our poor brains become hijacked again. For us to say *no* to the powerful products our brains have become trained to crave requires willpower. It's even harder to say no once we've been addicted to these products. The willpower required to detox and recover from addictions is significant. Occupied and exhausted, we stop paying attention to why we got addicted in the first place. We are too busy trying to survive.

Breaking free from the pleasure prison

But before we start playing the blame game, remember that all these companies are simply working the system. These companies have been created by the capitalist system. The system has created a cycle where we over-extract resources to produce goods we don't need, but that our brains have been hijacked to crave. Then we try to dispose of what's left of those now-unwanted goods to nature as waste.

We have created the paperclip nightmare scenario without the help of AI. Our unconscious primitive brains have been hijacked not by fear or threat, but by pleasure and our innate need and desire for it. It's all part of the meta-crisis.

Filling the spiritual void: Beyond mental health

All of this has led to a mental health crisis. We've created a society increasingly focused on individual gain over collective wellbeing. With no purpose, connection or meaning and stressed by societal expectations, environmental instability can easily trigger despair. If you're not at least a little depressed by reading this section, then you haven't fully understood the situation.

The result is a spiritual and existential void. Many of the world's religions teach us that we are unworthy, sinners from birth or conception. Even those of us who are not deeply religious swim in the belief soup of guilt, shame and unworthiness. We try to hide the disgusting self we have been taught to believe we are. We hide our struggle for love, worthiness and freedom through the accumulation of external possessions and material success. We strive to achieve the job, the house, the car, the clothes... We struggle to turn our perfectly lovely, healthy bodies into the impossible ideals of someone else's notion of beauty through diets, workouts, makeup and surgery. We are taught that we need these things if we are to be considered acceptable. Rampant materialism over meaning results in feelings of emptiness and lack of fulfilment. Why bother? Nothing matters. Empathy, compassion and deeper meaning are at risk of being jettisoned. Without community and connection, we lose our sense of belonging and our ethical and moral compass. We face a crisis of meaning of who we even are as a species and individuals.

Spiritual pain

If you've read this far and have allowed yourself to be aware of all we have lost (or are on the cusp of losing) as a culture, you are likely in pain. You might be feeling discomfort, despair, depression, hopelessness, anger, fear, hurt, resentment and grief. If you have fully understood the previous sections, you know there's a lot at stake, but it's OK. Your pain is the planet's pain. We are at our conscious tipping point of the planet and the pain you feel is spiritual.

Am I in spiritual pain?

Physical pain is simple. If you break your arm or get sick, the pain you feel is your body's message telling you something needs your attention. You may need medical attention; you almost certainly need to heal and rest.

Emotional pain is a little more nuanced and we experience it in two ways: we can feel pain in the present from something that happened in the past. We can also feel pain in the present from something happening in the present. If it's the latter, your pain is information. It's like a signal, telling you that you might be moving away from what you truly desire in life or moving towards what you don't desire. We can also feel pain in the present when someone crosses a boundary. This form of emotional pain simply tells you to take or stop some kind of action.

If the pain you feel is the result of past events, we call that trauma. Simply put, events from your past have created a resistance to love in your nervous system, and that feels painful (because it is). After being trafficked as a child and kept as a virtual house prisoner for five years, trauma is something I know a little about. I attempted to heal after my escape, which led me to create a tool to heal trauma. I call that tool Conscious Emotional Transformation (CET). CET is a psycho-spiritual process that heals all and any trauma from the past. It accomplishes in a matter of hours what other therapies might take years to heal. For a full explanation of the sources of emotional pain and how you can use CET to release yourself from emotional pain, you might like to read my book, *CET Yourself Free: Change your life with the gentle alchemy of Conscious Emotional Transformation.*[9] In the process of discovering Conscious Emotional Freedom, I found something else. I discovered the secret to healing not only emotional pain but also spiritual pain.

Spiritual pain is the pain you feel when you are disconnected from your source and your purpose. Spiritual pain is the pain you feel when you awaken spiritually and see the world but still feel powerless to change it. Spiritual pain is the pain we feel when we've left behind the old models, our past identity and old ways of being in and experiencing the world before we know who we are or we have the skills, resilience and consciousness to create the new, and, as we reach our conscious tipping point, that pain is heightened.

So, how can you identify and understand the pain you're in? You know it's not physical pain, and you might be tempted to believe it's emotional pain. In part, it is, but how can you know if the pain you're experiencing is spiritual?

Do you feel pain when you survey the world and all its suffering, and feel the suffering as if it was your own? Do you yearn for things to be different, but feel powerless to make any real changes? Do you retreat from the world as a result? Do you find a safe place where you can insulate and separate yourself from the pain and suffering of a world you feel incapable of changing? If so, you may be in spiritual pain. It's the misery you feel when you're not living your purpose. Your spiritual pain is part of living through our current moment of meta-crisis. Spiritual pain is both a symptom of the meta-crisis and one of its causes.

Let me explain. We've seen that the meta-crisis is the widespread, fundamental dysfunction of all the systems of our society affecting individuals and the viability of human existence. Now we understand that we feel spiritual pain when we are disconnected from our purpose, from meaning, from each other. The global challenges are so huge and seemingly unsolvable by any one individual that we are left feeling helpless in a hopeless situation – in other words, in spiritual pain.

And because we are in spiritual pain, feeling helpless and hopeless, we begin to ask ourselves, 'What is the point of caring? Why bother picking up my litter when everyone else litters? If everyone else is burning oil to travel for work, I might as well, too.' We think, 'My small part makes no difference, so we might as well go to the Bahamas for one last hurrah before we all burn.' The mother who needs to feed the babies doesn't have time or energy to care about how the factory that makes her baby's formula damages the planet. 'My baby is crying and must be fed,' is the only imperative she can know. Forced into survival thinking and feelings, we stop supporting and caring for each other. At our worst, we start attacking each other.

It's when we raise consciousness and reconnect to ourselves, our source, our Higher Self and each other, that we can evolve into deepened empathy and understanding, re-establishing a sense of shared hope and purpose. Through our connection to the source, we can all, collectively, start to prioritise the whole without sacrificing the individual. We see how the needs of the many don't sacrifice the individual, nor do the needs of the one sacrifice the collective. We are one and we are all.

So, what's the answer? Some people may claim that the pain we are experiencing, as individuals and as a species, is a sign that we are headed towards utopia or dystopia. I have a different take...

Utopia or dystopia

In thermodynamics and systems theory, there is a theory that states that a system will evolve to a greater level of complexity until its internal systems can no longer sustain themselves. At this point, known as the bifurcation point, the system will do one of two things. It will break down and dissolve or evolve to a higher level or order. Depending on who you listen to, the meta-crisis means that we are headed for a bifurcation point of our own. Utopia or dystopia. Heaven or hell on Earth. Choose your imagery.

How do we know if we've reached our bifurcation point? Are we headed for utopia or dystopia? Is there anything in between? What happens next?

If you listen to some spiritual groups, they may tell you that the meta-crisis means a great awakening is coming (what that is and how it happens is not so clear; the language they use is vague and intangible). From what I can gather, it seems that we, as a species, will suddenly and spontaneously 'awaken' and, after a short period of confusion, we will reorient ourselves and miraculously realise that all we need is love. If we are tolerant, kind and share nicely, all our ills will disappear. We will all live in blissful peace and harmony. Utopia!

The utopia described by these awakening believers is not only unfeasible, it's undesirable. The yearning for this kind of peace might sound nice, but it would make most of us miserable. This particular vision of peace is a form of toxic spirituality – seekers of this peace are looking for an escape, a way out from a world that doesn't work for them. Those who have experienced trauma but have not yet fully healed want to create a 'safe space' – but also a space without growth or change. What they call utopia would look like the end of evolution and learning, all that it is to be a seeking, growing human individual and species.

If you listen to others, you might hear that the meta-crisis is a sign of the coming apocalypse. The rich, elites and our governments are conspiring against the masses to control, manipulate and essentially enslave most of humanity for their own ends. They read the economic, emotional and legal oppressions many of us are experiencing as signs that others are attempting to suppress our awakening and empowerment. The 'preppers' worry about and plan for total systems failure, stockpiling dry goods and learning how to hunt and prepare their own food. Dystopia.

So, which is it, Lisa? Utopia or dystopia? Which is the natural outcome of the meta-crisis? I think neither is likely. Because utopia and dystopia are already here. Now. Poorer people in poorer places already live in toxic, ecologically ravaged places, with barely enough food, little sanitation or medical care, while the richest people in the richest places live in comparative luxury (speaking as a fortunate, wealthy person).

For large parts of the affluent, developed world, the majority of people have more than enough. What they describe as lack isn't lack of their needs being met, but lack of their desires being met – and wow, do they have desires. These desires are dressed up as needs. The desire for a bigger house, nicer car, fancier clothes and a new iPhone every year. However, these desires mask their deep need for admiration and validation, to fill the unmet needs of feeling not good enough on the inside with fancy stuff and a certain lifestyle. A world where any desire can be met becomes not utopia, but dystopia.

Envisioning Enlightopia

But like Pandora's box, we do have hope. There *is* a way through the meta-crisis that doesn't involve flawed visions of utopia or dystopia. If we look at the big picture of humanity and human progress, the data suggest that even though each excess of PowerCentre has brought challenges, on the whole, as we've activated our PowerCentres and moved up the energetic chain, things have, for the most part, gotten better for humanity. If we look at society before and after each PowerCentre was activated, it's pretty clear that things were better after each activation. Yes, activations led to excesses, which have, in turn, introduced new social problems. We've been living with many of these problems for decades now. The difference is that we are now poised to embrace a greater awareness of the meta-crisis. With greater awareness, as uncomfortable as it might be, we can take action to change things. Overall, as humanity, both collectively and as individuals, has become more conscious and more aware, we've created growth for the greater good.

We can move from an ego-centric to an eco-centric perspective. We can do this by understanding the interconnectedness of all life and embracing a philosophy that values the collective good alongside individual freedoms. We can do this by celebrating our differences and uniqueness through love, compassion and critical thinking. We can do this by finding meaning in solving this.

Here's some good news. Every single one of us has a brilliant brain. A brain that is designed to think and problem-solve. If we each put our consciousness into tackling our small or great part of the meta-crisis, we can make a difference. We can not only survive but thrive.

At the core of this model is the evolution of consciousness. The awakening to the interconnectedness of all life and the realisation of our collective power to shape reality. The word evolution refers to our biological evolution, the physical development of our bodies to their current form, beyond the evolution and expansion of our intellect and consciousness.

Our physical bodies evolved. Our minds and intellects evolved. Our society and culture evolved to support and sustain the growth of both of these. We cannot stop evolution. We will always be evolving and it could be said that we have already evolved beyond our environment.

Thus far our growth has been physical, emotional and intellectual. As we come up to hitting all the planetary boundaries of resources, we still crave growth, but that growth is what will kill us and our planet.

What if there was a way to grow, that actually *saves* our planet? When we ask the question, are we heading for utopia or dystopia? There is another possibility. Utopia is a society where everything works perfectly to sustain our physical needs. Dystopia is the opposite. Rather than focusing on just these as two possible routes, there might be a third way. Enlightopia. Yes, I made that word up. Enlightopia means, rather than focusing on external material needs and growth, that evolution takes place within. Within every individual, and also within the inner landscape of humanity and our consciousness itself.

Enlightopia, where the emphasis is on growing internally, expanding the self and moving the focus from generating monetary wealth to generating spiritual wealth. This society supports the ideals of enlightened consciousness, spiritual growth, wisdom and interconnectedness all integrated into the fabric of everyday life. Just as one is expected to eat, shower and brush our teeth daily, consciousness-raising practices are embedded in our individual and collective daily lives.

As the Crown chakra activates, we can expect to move from consumerism to compassion. From possessions to presences, from currency to consciousness and from wallets to wisdom. We must choose to change ourselves and our culture. We must choose to change what we value and how we demonstrate that value. We need a world where we prioritise our energy, harnessing it to make the world a better place for all, not just the few. We need to remember that the needs of the many outweigh the needs of the one. Transcendence is the answer, and coming up: how to do it!

Summary

- We have become unconsciously addicted to synthetic replacements for natural human needs, leading to a cycle of consumption driven by corporate interests.

- The addiction to pleasure, whether through food, social media or consumer products, has created a spiritual void and mental health crisis, leaving individuals feeling disconnected and without purpose.

- The current systems encourage overconsumption and exploitation, resulting in environmental degradation and a cycle of addiction to products that do not fulfil genuine human needs.

- The paperclip nightmare scenario illustrates how an unchecked system can lead to a singular focus on production without regard to necessity or consequence.

- Addressing the meta-crisis requires transcending individual desires for collective wellbeing and embracing a shift towards spiritual growth and interconnectedness, moving from a consumer-based society to one focused on consciousness and compassion.

SELF-REFLECTION QUESTIONS FOR DEEPER EXPLORATION

1. How do your personal consumption habits contribute to the cycle of addiction and exploitation described in the chapter?

2. Have you experienced anything similar to the spiritual void mentioned? What steps can you take to reconnect with a deeper sense of purpose?

3. How could you contribute to shifting society from a focus on material wealth to spiritual growth and interconnectedness?

4. What actions can you take to prioritise collective wellbeing over individual desires in your community and beyond, without sacrificing yourself?

7
Meta-Crisis To Meta-Cause

What must we do to move from the meta-crisis to a meta-cause and our conscious tipping point? What are we called to do to achieve collective transcendence? This chapter considers the steps we can each take to achieve the next cultural shift – a transformation from a society ensnared in materialism and disconnection to one thriving in conscious awareness and harmonious coexistence.

We know how bad things are and how much worse it could become if we don't change course. It's not hopeless, and you're not helpless. We'll discover that the key to transcending our meta-crisis lies within each of us. Together, we'll envision a future where humanity's collective consciousness evolves to create a world of balance, equality and unity.

Then, we'll explore the tangible, practical actions we can all start to take to make conscious culture our reality. We'll meet a future highly evolved being from another dimension or timeline who has already achieved this along the way. They'll give us the inspiration we need to move forward.

Conscious culture creation

The evolution of our collective consciousness is like that of a child maturing to adulthood. We started with childlike curiosity and experimentation. With a sense of wonder, we took our initial forays into technology, driven by curiosity and the desire to explore new possibilities. Children have limited awareness; their consciousness is often only able to manage black-and-white thinking, right and wrong, good and bad. Just as a child can't comprehend nuances, context and complexity, we as a species haven't yet managed to fully embody these qualities.

Just as adolescents can be prone to making reckless, rebellious choices that have short- and long-term consequences for their lives (and the lives of others), as a species, we've tended to be stubborn and wilfully ignorant, and made choices without thinking through the consequences of our actions. However, as fully conscious, highly aware adults, our culture would expand to embrace a deeper awareness of our actions and how they impact others and our environment.

When we live as a highly conscious society that has successfully transcended the meta-crisis, we'd find ourselves in a world where advanced technology, elevated consciousness and a profound connection to all forms of life coexist in a state of balance and harmony.

I'm going to offer an imaginative glimpse into what this might look like. However, what I'm not going to do is offer structural details as to how we might achieve this world. I'm not a policy-maker. In what follows, I am deliberately staying away from politics, policies and laws. Not only are these areas not my expertise, but I also don't think that we necessarily have the answers to the policy questions plaguing our species – yet. We do know what the desired results from big policy changes could look like, and I do know that now is the time for individuals to consciously awaken to help lead those big-level changes and drive the policies that will get us where we want to go.

If humanity succeeds in raising its collective consciousness, the potential outcomes are profoundly positive and transformative. Here is how we might live.

A message from the future

Imagine if you will, a future where we are living in a transcendent culture. Or, if you prefer, you can pretend that a highly evolved being from the future has returned to us in the here and now to share with us how we transcended the meta-crisis and give us a glimpse of what a transcendent future looks like.

Collective consciousness: Every thought, word, intention and action impact the resonant field of the whole and will influence it. As such, we are careful with our thoughts, both conscious and unconscious. In a transcendent culture, we embody a state of higher consciousness, where empathy, compassion and understanding are automatically embedded in every interaction and decision.

Interconnectedness: We have a deep sense of the interconnectedness of all life, beings, people and peoples on Earth. We know our actions have conse-quences beyond ourselves and our locale. We make all our decisions and base all our actions on the sense and knowing that what we do impacts everyone and everything. Conflicts are resolved by making deci-sions for the highest good of *all*. We know that when one group is marginalised or disadvantaged, we are creating more problems in the longer term.

Emotional intelligence: We are living in a world where compassion goes beyond simply being nice to everyone. We use emotional intelligence. We approach others with compassion and a desire to understand and support, rather than to punish and penalise. We understand that when someone behaves in a way that damages themselves or others, the intention is rarely to damage, but usually to get a need met, such as love, self-worth, belonging, autonomy or competency. We find ways to help individuals create, love and grow. We avoid ego and the power dynamics that are so destructive and self-limiting. We advocate for transparency and honesty. We can do this because we've let go of judgement. By knowing and expressing who we are and what we are attempting to achieve in a forum of acceptance and nonjudgement, all may seek to get their needs and desires met in healthy and empowering ways.

Ecological restoration and harmony: We are aware of the interconnectedness of all life, and this knowing drives us to more sustainable living and policies, reversing environmental degradation and fostering a harmonious relationship with nature.

We coexist with nature. Our civilisation now lives in complete harmony with our planet's ecosystems. We continually develop technology and lifestyles that enhance rather than deplete the environment. Nature is revered, loved and protected, not as a provider of resources or as somewhere to dump our waste, but for its intrinsic beauty and goodness. We live the truth that for the health, survival and thriving of all, we need nature.

Technological advancement for the greater good: Technology is used ethically and responsibly, focusing on solving global challenges, enhancing quality of life and promoting learning and exploration. We embrace advanced but sustainable technologies. Rather than trying to go back to low tech and high nature, or marching blindly towards low nature and high tech, we now live in a culture of high tech working alongside and with nature. This includes the sustainable production and use of energy. We aim to only use materials that are biodegradable and recyclable. If this is not yet possible, we use materials minimally and take steps to account for environmental impact, both locally and globally.

Social and economic equality: Elevated consciousness nurtures systems based on fairness, equality, shared prosperity, reducing poverty and inequality and ensuring basic needs are met for all. If no one goes without, they do not need to fight, or create war or unrest to get their basic needs met, ensuring that our Base PowerCentre remains open, active and balanced.

With resources distributed effectively, everyone has enough to live a fulfilling life. Freed from poverty, penury and debt, we have more time to turn our energy and brainpower to work for the greater good. We move from wallets to wisdom. From pursuing profits to cultivating consciousness. This isn't socialism or communism. We've created something entirely new and equitable, something we might eventually call 'conscious capitalism'.

Global peace and cooperation: A collective consciousness shift fosters a sense of global community, leading to peaceful resolutions of conflicts, cooperative international relations and a focus on common human interests. In a conscious culture, we are acutely aware of the interconnectedness of all things, all systems and all people and peoples. We all rise or we all fall.

Inner instead of outer growth: We have shifted from outer to inner growth. In the past, pre-transcendence, we defined value and importance as wealth, possessions, status, physical beauty and power. We pursued these things to feel valued and loved, but now we've made the shift from valuing outer appearances to valuing inner growth. We do not need to impress others to feel good about ourselves. We seek inner fulfilment and the expression of our purpose, empowering all and being useful beyond the individual.

True change comes from within. We pursue personal growth and self-awareness as fundamental to creating a better world. As we evolve as individuals, we create a better society. We celebrate the development of individual, intrinsic joy and happiness as we cultivate an environment where individuals can hone and perfect skills, knowledge and inner growth. When people find intrinsic joy in doing something rather than from the results they get from doing it, they do not need external recognition or validation. When individuals are celebrated, respected and rewarded for bettering themselves, for learning and growing and developing, they *choose to* enthusiastically give back to society.

Holistic education and lifelong learning: We celebrate and value education. We are always seeking new information, knowledge and insights. We have no fear of being 'wrong' and no one has imposter syndrome. In a transcendent culture, no one is judged for believing what old evidence tells them. Not only is education and knowledge valued, but it is also freely and easily available to all. Education is understood as a lifelong journey, with an equal emphasis on intellectual development and emotional and spiritual growth. We seek wisdom, not merely knowledge, so we can ensure that knowledge is used for the highest good. Critical thinking is celebrated and enjoyed.

Cultural diversity and exchange: A deeper appreciation for diverse cultures arises, leading to a robust exchange of ideas, traditions and knowledge, enriching the global culture. A transcendent culture is rich in arts, music and creative expression, celebrating the diversity and depth of our experiences.

Innovation and creativity: As consciousness rises, so does creativity and innovation, leading to breakthroughs in arts, sciences and various fields of human endeavour.

Mental and emotional wellbeing: As people find more meaning and connection in their lives, mental health improves, leading to a more empathetic, compassionate society.

Health and longevity: The health system and compensation for providing health is based on wellness rather than illness. We hone and continually work towards holistic approaches to health. We integrate physical, mental and spiritual wellbeing. As a result, we have greatly extended not only our lifespans but our flourishing lifespans. Overall quality of life is improved for all.

Democratic and inclusive governance: Political systems become more inclusive, transparent and participatory, reflecting the collective will and best interests of the populace. Transcendent governance is based on wisdom, fairness and inclusion, rather than power or competition or mob rule. Leaders demonstrate deep understanding and compassion. With a highly educated and proactively informed public, democracy is more nuanced and functional. Individuals consider not only their own needs and desires but the needs and desires of the greater good for the longer term.

Sustainable and equitable economic systems: Transcendent economic systems are centred on wellbeing, the highest good of all, at the expense and sacrifice of none. All systems, decisions and actions balance the long- and short-term wellbeing of the whole society and our planet. Economies evolve to focus on sustainable practices, equitable distribution of resources and long-term wellbeing over short-term gains.

Spiritual and philosophical renaissance: A renewed interest in spirituality and philosophy leads to diverse explorations of meaning, purpose and connection, enriching human experience and understanding. At the heart of transcendence is spiritual fulfilment, which is deeply integrated into our lives, providing a sense of connection to all. We recognise that we are all connected. We are united, but also unique. We celebrate differences and diversity and peacefully exchange wisdom, knowledge and joy with other civilisations.

Interstellar exploration and cooperation: With a more unified and peaceful Earth, humanity turns its eyes to the stars, not for conquest, but for knowledge and peaceful exploration. We have an interdimensional understanding. We interact with the multidimensional nature of the universe. We recognise that our past is important because it is what enabled us to become who we have become. In short, transcending our conscious tipping point is what led to the beauty we enjoy every day.

Oh, and we travel through time and space... OK, that last bit might be a bit of a stretch – but what if? To make this future a reality, we need to come from a place of 'What if?' The 'What if?' question opens up possibilities.

This vision for our planet isn't only a dream; it is a potential future that can be guided by the collective actions and evolution of humanity. Raising consciousness is not merely an abstract concept, but a practical pathway to a future where humanity thrives in harmony with each other and the planet. It requires individual and collective effort and a willingness to learn, grow and embrace change.

The challenge is that we can't make others awaken. We can't force others to raise their consciousness to be better. We can't force the collective to awaken and raise our cultural consciousness. We can only do this for ourselves. We need to lead from here and now. *We* are the leaders we have been waiting for. *We* are the changemakers we have been hoping for. *We* are the ones who will save ourselves. It starts with us. It starts with you. It starts with me.

Summary

- We face multiple challenges which we can overcome with transcendence to a higher level of thinking and being. As individuals, we must remain hopeful and harness our power to change our future.

- Our best hope is a cultural shift towards a conscious creation of a transcendent culture.

- We are currently in a technological adolescence stage – we have the power to destroy without yet

127

having the wisdom to create something better for all.

- The move to a transcendent culture where technology, consciousness and nature harmoniously coexist is a desirable outcome for all – and possible.

- A message from a highly evolved being from the future shows the potential of a transcendent culture.

- A transcendent future might entail collective consciousness, interconnectedness, emotional intelligence, ecological harmony, technological advancement for the greater good, social and economic equality, global peace and cooperation and the shift from external to internal growth.

- This is a call to action for individuals to awaken and lead the transformation towards a conscious society.

SELF-REFLECTION QUESTIONS FOR DEEPER EXPLORATION

1. What aspects of a transcendent culture most resonate with you, and how can you embody these qualities in your daily life?

2. What aspects of a transcendent culture are not listed in this chapter that you would like to see created?

3. What aspects of a transcendent culture as described would you struggle to embrace? Why?

4. In what ways can you foster deeper emotional intelligence, wisdom, critical thinking and compassion in your interactions with others?

5. Consider your personal growth journey. How can you prioritise inner growth over external achievements to contribute to a conscious society?

8

Why We Aren't There Yet: Understanding Our Evolutionary Blockages

If we know what to do and how wonderful it would be when we do it, why are we not there yet? Why are we still trapped in the same old cycles and systems? Why have we not changed? Could it be that we have been using the wrong map, model or tools?

The good news is that there is a model which I've been using with individuals and small groups for many years now. It seems to work, but only if you know how to use it. You're going to discover the exact and simple steps to take for you to awaken and some of the stumbling blocks on the path to enlightenment. We'll reveal why some of the things that feel so good about awakening, can actually be traps if we're not wise to them.

We won't only ask why we haven't realised our collective vision for a better world and our own spiritual awakening; I'll also show you a map of the obstacles that hold us back. With the right map, tools and techniques, we can all experience and reach transcendence.

From vision to reality: Navigating our collective awakening

The world I've just described sounds pretty good, right? If I've done my job, I've hopefully described the world that your soul has been yearning for. It's a world that you want to live in. I hope it's a world that you'll willing to help create. With me, and with others who have embraced their transcendent awakening to become conscious culture creators. More on how you (and all of us) can actually do that soon. First, I want to address one of the common questions that comes up when I share my vision of an awakened world with others.

Typically, when I talk about 'conscious culture creation', my audiences get excited. They are inspired. The vision of the world that I've laid before them is one that they've been craving. They may have been sharing some of the same thoughts and visions. In this possible future, they feel seen, but they are also curious. 'Lisa,' they ask me, 'if we know what we need to create a future that supports the needs of the many over the needs of the one, why haven't we done it yet? Why aren't we there yet?' To understand how we evolve consciously and awake spiritually, we need to understand a little of how our minds work.

The mechanics of the soul: Our three minds

We can think of our consciousness (soul, being, essence) as not one thing, but existing in three parts: the conscious mind, the unconscious mind and the Higher Self. Although I use the word 'mind', I am not referring to the brain in an anatomical or physiological way (even though our brain plays a central part in storing information and emotions). I'm not suggesting that your brain has only three parts. When I use 'mind', I mean the levels of awareness that make up our psyche. It's important to note that these are *not* three separate entities, but rather three distinct aspects of your whole being and awareness. Each of these minds is a mode of thinking.

The Three Minds

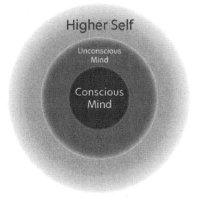

1. **Conscious mind:** The conscious mind is the part of us that experiences reality; it's also the part of us that chooses and decides what's real. Our conscious mind is everything we pay attention to in our present moment of awareness. It allows us to focus and concentrate – it is the home of rational thought, judgements, decisions and assessments. It is our free will. The conscious mind isn't fixed; our present moment of awareness can change at any moment and can move between our past (memories), our immediate present moment and our future (hopes, dreams, fears, etc).

2. **Unconscious mind:** Our unconscious mind is everything else or everything that we are *not* currently conscious of. Our unconscious mind contains our personal programming, beliefs and patterns, emotional blueprints, strategies and skills. While these things are usually completely outside of our conscious awareness, we live their effects in our choices, beliefs and behaviours. Memories and emotions reside in the unconscious mind, including unresolved emotions from the past and trauma.

3. **Higher Self:** Our Higher Self is the part of us that is pure source/love/divine. Inspiration and intuition flow from the Higher Self. You *are* your Higher Self, expressing itself through the lens of *your* personality in physical form.

A human is the integration of all three minds functioning optimally together. Thus, you are infinite. You are your Infinite Higher Self, expressing itself through your unconscious mind, consciously aware of yourself via your conscious mind. (This is a *huge* concept that I explain in detail in my other books and courses if you want to learn more.)

The three minds integrated

Simply, integrating our three minds takes work. Many of us can get stuck along the way. This happens because of the relationship between the conscious mind, unconscious mind and Higher Self. Before we can understand how we can open our conscious and unconscious minds to the beautiful, divine and blissful flow of energy from our Higher Self, we have to understand how and why those connections get blocked.

The conscious mind and Higher Self are separated by the barrier or buffer of the unconscious mind. The unconscious mind acts as the conduit or pathway for insights, wisdom and information. Here lies the problem. The conscious mind has access to the unconscious mind, but that access can be limited. Some memories, thoughts and ideas are not readily accessible by the conscious mind. Techniques such as mindfulness, meditation, dreamwork, hypnosis and trance work can help increase our conscious access to the depths of the unconscious. When we increase our ability to access our unconscious mind, we can be more resourceful, our memory improves and we can become more creative.

What's the problem, you might be asking right now. Aren't increased memory power and creativity good things? Important things? Useful things? Yes! At this stage of awakening, we can develop some astonishing spiritual powers. We might start to experience phenomena such as speaking to past loved ones, perceiving energy and auras and even experiences that seem like telepathy and other near-magical powers. Again, how is this a problem? Because there is more – so much more.

Connecting the conscious and unconscious minds: Potential and pitfalls

The abilities we can hone and develop when we increase the connection between the conscious and unconscious minds are so enchanting that we can get stuck here. All of these new powers are fascinating, but they are limited in one specific way – *they are all based on information that is already known*. Remember, the unconscious mind can store a vast amount of information. The limitation is that it can only store information that is already known. None of the information lurking in its depths is new or original.

For example, we store all of our biases, fears, restrictions and limiting beliefs in our unconscious mind. When we open the connection between our conscious and unconscious minds, we open ourselves up to new spiritual experiences and gifts. However, when we experience an intense and profound state (a vision-inducing, ecstasy-activating state), it can be so intense and all-encompassing that it temporarily masks our shortcomings, our blocks, our fears and our limitations. I call this being 'stuck at enchantment'. And it's one reason why we, as individuals and as a species, have yet to fully awaken and evolve. A change of state is temporary, but evolution, growth and expansion are permanent.

Stuck at enchantment

Being stuck at enchantment is common and an easy trap to fall into. A newly awakened person can be so overwhelmed by new feelings of compassion, connection, bliss and ecstasy that they mistake these intense feelings for signs of their spiritual uniqueness. They leap to the conclusion that there is something about *them*, as opposed to something special about the experience. Their unconscious mind empties all of its biases, patterns and limiting beliefs into the conscious mind, which interprets the experience as a sign that the individual has been 'called' to something greater. Often, these individuals believe that, now that they are awakened, it is their job to awaken everyone else. They become the sanctimonious do-gooder. Rather than leading us to explore, learn and discover for ourselves, they tell us to follow them blindly.

People stuck in enchantment can become obsessed with trying to replicate and repeat the bliss, the ecstasy or the vision, and they want to guide others to the same experience. They chase the state, rather than chasing deeper expansion. Unfortunately, because these individuals haven't completed the full cycle of awakening, they still have healing to do. Instead of seeing a spiritual experience for what it is – a step along the way to true evolution – they become obsessed with the idea that they've already arrived. Instead of doing more work, they chase the bliss.

They avoid triggers or any experience or encounter that would challenge their belief that they've already 'arrived' at spiritual bliss, nirvana, transcendence, etc. They become obsessed with protecting themselves from spiritual and emotional 'threats' that might challenge the identity they've created for themselves. They become driven by fear, craving an escape from the real-world problems that, without access to their bliss state, they can't handle or cope with. They deny what's happening in the real world or believe they will be saved from any harsh effects of the meta-crisis because they are one of the chosen. They become the 'Pollyanna pessimists'. 'Everyone is doomed but we will be saved.' There's no need for further change, just follow the 'bliss-fuck' to redemption. That's how many of us get stuck.

Stuck without therapeutics

When we awaken, the first thing that happens is that we raise our awareness. We become aware of the 'contents' of our unconscious mind. We begin to parse our patterns and behaviours, our pain and our trauma. This is a good thing that seems like a bad thing. Imagine going into the attic or that box room filled with clutter and pulling it all out. Once it's out, now you have all of this *stuff* all over your house. You have to do something with it. However, what if we don't have the tools? We need boxes to pack the stuff up and a trailer to take it to the tip. We need the discernment to decide what is junk and what are jewels. This is the cause of some of the toxicity in spirituality.

Typically, ancient spiritual traditions offered us the discernment and tools we need to sort the junk from the jewels, to help us complete our processes of spiritual awakening. Ancient spiritual traditions generally had some form of what spirituality calls 'therapeutics': a mentor, guru, shaman, ascended master or mage who had been through the programme, learned the lessons and was now able to act as a guide to others. Now, however, with spiritual knowledge readily available from the likes of TikTok, but without the therapeutics to guide us through the whole process of trauma healing by sharing the wisdom we need to discern the jewels from the junk, we have no tools or skills for handling our spiritual pain. Therefore, we will deny it, hide from it and paint over it with positivity – all the things that toxic spirituality mandates us to do/feel/be/buy. This is another way individuals attempting to connect their conscious and unconscious minds get stuck along the way and are unable to evolve into connecting the Higher Self.

The illusion of arrival: The potential and pitfalls of the Higher Self

Not everyone becomes stuck at enchantment or stuck without therapeutics. Those who heal their unconscious trauma, blocks and limitations free themselves to move along to the next level of awakening and evolution. They are accessing their Higher Selves, focusing on aligning the Higher Self and unconscious mind. This is a powerful, purposeful and compelling place to be in our spiritual evolution.

When we become aligned with our Higher Self, we have access to new individual and collective insights. In this phase, intuition is high, strong and trusted. The aligned no longer fear emotions; they understand them as feedback. When they are triggered by a new pocket of pain, they simply do the work to heal it. They are compassionate and will never harm another. They've moved beyond the fascinating spiritual phenomenon that can trap those who stay stuck in enchantment. They understand that phenomena are simply a side effect of spiritual development, not spiritual development itself. Abilities such as speaking to the dead become interesting and intriguing, but rarely useful.

Stuck at enlightenment

At this level of spiritual evolution, we are fully aware of our soul's purpose and what we desire to embody in our physical reality. We do what is necessary for us to express our true purpose. We do the training, get the skills, read the books and take the courses – joyfully. We will do it not for the money or other rewards but simply because it brings joy. We find it easy to access flow states here because we simply love what we do. These flow states are similar to the ecstatic state, but because they are internally generated, we don't experience the same *crash* when we exit them. For example, we can enter flow states via external stimuli, such as psychotropic substances, a particular location or via a brain entrainment system. However, because these external factors are outside of our control, we can experience a 'crash' when we exit them (or are kicked out of them when the drug wears off, or the device powers down, etc). However, when we learn to enter flow states and ecstatic states at will, via our own internally governed strategies, we can enter and leave them, and exit them we must. No one can be in flow all the time and the aligned being knows this and accepts this. However, it's possible to become stuck here, too. While aligned beings might be and embody all these good things, they may not do much good. Let me explain.

Those who become stuck in this phase of their spiritual evolution tend to be a bit self-serving. True, they are living their own purpose but they may not yet have the desire to serve the greater good. They may seek the luxury lifestyle but recycle along the way. Think of the entrepreneur who makes a lot of money doing what they love (great for them) but they may not be making much of a difference to others, to the world. Therefore, although they don't actively harm anyone, they don't do much good either. At some point, these people (and maybe this is you, right now) may feel called to something. They have a niggling sense they could do more and be more. They want to move beyond individual purpose-led alignment to a collective purpose-led alignment. Because, yes, there is a level of spiritual evolution beyond the Higher Self. We call this transcendence.

Transcendence

Transcendence is the experience of going beyond yourself and your limitations. It means connecting with and expressing yourself from a higher perspective. We can access the unconscious mind and then go further to our Higher Self, but it is also possible to go even further, beyond the individual, to experience the perspective of the *collective* Higher Self. The collective Higher Self might refer to a group, a country, an organisation or even the entire species.

Transcendence might first be experienced as a state that you enter. Like a flow state or an ecstatic state, it is wonderful. However, transcendence has the added dimension of profound change. The New Age guru might call this going beyond the third dimension to the fifth or ninth dimension, or something similar. This is a useful metaphor, and we can use it as such. We move from one who has experienced a transcendent state to someone who can be called a transcendent being when we can access this state on demand but without addiction or attachment. I like to call transcendent beings transcendents.

If we decide that an awakened conscious culture is worth creating and that we are willing to do what is necessary to make that happen, then it's up to all of us. We all have a role to play. Every individual needs to live as a transcendent being. A transcendent being:

- Is someone joyful, productive, helpful, supportive, loving, compassionate and sincere

- Lives their life as a work of art

- Doesn't seek inner peace; they have inner peace because they have inner strength

- Has moved beyond the restrictions of ego and has access to a higher perspective

- Has realised their true nature and purpose, far beyond lifestyle or adding value, making money or being powerful

- Has a healthy ego; they know who they are and use their skills and insights to create pragmatic change in the world

- Doesn't wait to be saved; they work to save themselves, but they also inspire others to save themselves

Those who do this are the changemakers, the loving leaders. They are powerful and purpose-led. They are loving. We can be the changemakers, the loving leaders. We can be powerful and purpose-led. We can be loving. Are you ready?

Summary

- Spiritual awakening is easier and more foolproof when you understand how the mind works, and the mechanics of the psyche.

- Our minds have three modes of working: the conscious mind, the unconscious mind and the Higher Self.

- Integrating our three minds requires techniques, and many of us can get stuck along the way.

- The unconscious mind acts as a conduit for insights from the Higher Self, but blocks, trauma, painful emotions or limiting beliefs can limit access to new insights from the Higher Self.

- Spiritual experiences can be intense and mask our shortcomings, leading to becoming 'stuck at enchantment'.

- Enhancing the connection between the conscious and unconscious minds can unlock spiritual powers, but also present limitations.

- Fully aligning with the Higher Self allows for greater individual and collective insights, moving beyond mere spiritual phenomena.

- Transcendence involves connecting with and expressing from a higher perspective, going beyond individual limitations to embrace collective consciousness.

SELF-REFLECTION QUESTIONS FOR DEEPER EXPLORATION

1. Have you ever been seduced by enchantment and been tempted to stay at this level? How can you recognise when you're being held there? What steps can you take to move beyond this stage?

2. Reflect on the tools and practices you currently use to access your unconscious mind. How can you deepen this connection to facilitate your spiritual growth?

3. Consider your relationship with your Higher Self. How do you cultivate this connection, and what

barriers do you encounter in aligning with it more fully?

4. In what ways can you contribute to a collective awakening, moving beyond individual evolution towards embracing our shared purpose?

5. Transcendence involves going beyond personal limitations. How do you envision your role in creating a conscious culture that transcends current societal challenges?

9
The Cycle Of Transcendent Awakening

Although the saying, 'It's not about the destination, it's about the journey,' isn't usually applied to goals, it's perfect to apply to our lives as a whole. Let's face it – the destination of life is, well… death, but that's not the purpose or meaning of life. (I promise I'm a hoot in real life and not this grim!) If there is a purpose to our individual lives and the existence of humanity as a whole, it seems likely that it's to evolve – to grow and have some fun experiences on the way.

Could the purpose of life be to become more aware, to become more conscious, to raise our consciousness and increase our understanding and awareness of ourselves, to know our place in the world and universe, as well as the role or roles we play when interacting with others? It could also be to simply experience more and more. Is it possible that the more we experience, the more we *evolve*?

We see cycles everywhere in nature. Systems, organisations and living beings are either growing or they are dying. By evolving, we increase life through our growth. If we are not evolving and growing, we are shrinking. Change and evolution require an expansion of awareness, accessing knowledge and wisdom while also letting go of what no longer serves us. Evolution is a journey, and all journeys are best undertaken with a map and some directions. Even journeys with no final destination are more fun if we know where we are and what we might expect next.

Every experience you have leaves its mark on your mind and neurology, so the question isn't, 'Can we change?' It's, 'How do we change into who we *want* to become, rather than randomly stumbling from one state to the next?'

The seven stages of transcendent awakening

All change happens as a process; we move from one state to another in stages. Evolution happens in a cycle with distinct stages – a pattern, if you like. I call this the cycle of transcendent awakening, which has seven distinct stages. Each brings its opportunities and joys, as well as its unique challenges. The good news is that once you understand the cycle of awakening, change becomes easy. When you know where you are in the cycle and what's coming next, transformation becomes easy, predictable and a lot more fun.

The most important thing to note is that the cycle of transcendent awakening is a cycle or spiral of evolution, not a ladder. The end of one cycle becomes the beginning of the next, at a higher level. There is no 'end'. We're never done. Each successive journey becomes more and more awakened and evolved while knowing that there's always more to learn. There are no limits, only levels. There is no 'awakened'. We are always awakening. The seven stages of transcendent awakening are shown below.

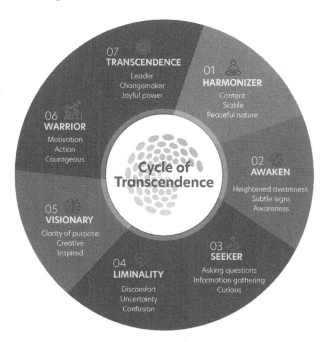

Before you read on to discover more about each stage, you might like to take a short quiz that will show you which stage you are currently at. You'll find it on our website: www.OCTPBook.com.

The harmoniser

At this stage, you're happy with how things are. You've achieved a level of stability that you are content with. You're willing to accept the status quo. Harmonisers may even fight to maintain it, preferring things to stay the same. Some harmonisers can even get trapped in a place of judgement rather than getting curious about why things are the way they are.

Some harmonisers will sacrifice their true calling and happiness just to keep the peace, but at what cost? Are you stuck at the harmoniser stage? Wanting things to stay the same and slipping into denial rather than honouring your deeper truths? It's OK if you're not quite ready to shake things up. You might want to change but feel too scared to rock the boat, or not know how to make it happen or have the courage yet.

When the harmonisers are no longer willing to settle and allow themselves to know that deep down they want more, that's when things start slowly, but surely, to shift. Eventually, though, all things change.

The awakening

Awakening often starts with those weird little signs, signals and feelings you begin to notice. Perhaps you feel that something isn't quite right, or you might intuitively know something is wrong. Your awareness becomes heightened and you might feel confused, or just curious.

Awakening starts with noticing things that don't quite seem to fit your current understanding or model of the world. You thought you knew how things worked, but strange things started to happen. You might just find yourself being surprised by people behaving in ways that you didn't expect, or perhaps strange coincidences keep happening. Perhaps the same numbers keep showing up, and similar messages repeat themselves. You feel differently about people and places and you don't quite know why.

You might have strange dreams or become increasingly sensitive to others, to people and places. You begin to question things. Why do things have to be this way? Isn't there more to life than this? Who says this is how it is? You start to question the status quo. You wonder if the things that you've always accepted as true are the way things are. Whereas at the harmoniser stage, everything has a box, and everything fits in a box, during the awakening stage, you start to find that some things don't fit in the boxes and you have no idea why, so you start asking questions.

You start to notice small signs, subtle and not-so-subtle, signals that things just don't seem to make sense the way they used to. What you were previously happy with no longer satisfies you. You start to want more. You wonder if there's more to life or if you have experiences that just don't make sense or fit into your beliefs.

You begin to ask questions, and it's these questions that cause you to seek answers. You notice changes in both yourself and others. You sense that you're different. You don't quite fit in anymore, nor are you sure you even want to. You experience raised awareness and increased self-awareness. When you get curious enough, or you just can't deny the bleedin' obvious, you start to seek answers.

The seeker

As soon as you start asking questions and demanding answers, you become a seeker. As a seeker, you have questions and you want answers. The seeker stage represents your transformative journey fuelled by unquenchable curiosity and an insatiable thirst for knowledge.

You are characterised by your open-mindedness, willingness to explore new ideas and profound desire for personal transformation. You embark on inner and outer adventures, questioning the status quo and seeking answers to life's deeper questions. Dissatisfied with conventional paradigms, you embrace change, developing clarity about your life's purpose and the need for alignment. With courage and resilience, you navigate the unsettling awareness that the old way of living no longer fits, integrating newfound wisdom and moving forward on a path of self-discovery and authenticity.

You actively seek out the knowledge you want. You ask questions; perhaps you read books and articles; you listen to podcasts and go to seminars and workshops. Eventually, you get enough information and understanding of your current situation and its challenges, issues and problems. You start to think about making changes in your life. However, you still don't quite know what to change or how to do it. You enter the no man's land of liminality.

Liminality

Liminality is that space between. You're not here but not there. You don't know where you're heading but can't go back either. It's like being stuck in a threshold between two rooms. It's tempting to try to rush out of the liminal place because the uncertainty can be so uncomfortable. Our minds love certainty, but you need to take a moment to pause and check where you're headed. You need to pause and reflect. You need to let go of what *was*, and then decide what *will be*.

One of the characteristics of liminality is this need to let go. It can be a time of grieving, sadness and regrets.

It's OK to feel these feelings. It's important that you do. Once you know what to let go of and where you are heading, you'll move to the next stage.

The liminal stage marks a pivotal and often dis-orienting phase in the evolutionary cycle. At this stage, you find yourself standing at the threshold of profound change, acutely aware that the old way of life, beliefs and paradigms no longer serve your evolving self. The doors of your past are closed, but you don't yet know which door to your future to open. Confronted with uncertainty, not knowing precisely what lies ahead, it's a time of letting go of the familiar, which can be unsettling and even chaotic.

You've outgrown your previous self and are in a state of transition, akin to the cocoon of a butterfly before it emerges transformed. This stage is charac-terised by ambiguity, a sense of being betwixt and between and a deep yearning for clarity and direc-tion. The discomfort of not knowing what's next or of not having a clear path forward is intense, but it is in this liminal space that profound shifts can occur, paving the way for a rebirth into a new way of being and becoming.

In liminality, you're forced to surrender and trust the process and embrace the unknown, as it holds the potential for profound growth and transformation.

Visionary

At the visionary stage, you start making active choices and plans. You'll hone and refine your dreams and visions. You'll start imagining your beautiful new life and way of being. You're creative and inspired and you find clarity of vision and purpose. However, you can't stay a dreamer forever. You have to make it happen, and that requires taking action.

As the visionary, you are a dreamer with a crystal-clear vision of an extraordinary future waiting to be realised. Fuelled by ambition and a strong sense of purpose, you hold the power to inspire and captivate those around you. With great leaps in understanding and creativity, you receive insights from higher realms, paving the way for remarkable transformations.

The visionary is often charismatic and driven by an inner calling. You hold the vision of a better life, a better world. You imagine, dream and make plans. The visionary needs to get absolute clarity about the vision. For your vision to become reality, you need to put the plans into place. Run the numbers and do the drawings. Make that spreadsheet. If it stays in your head, it will never become real.

Warrior

As soon as you start to actively build your vision, make changes and create and build something, you'll meet resistance. For your vision to be formed and become real, you'll need to fight for it. Others won't want you to change. Some might not like what you're creating. Some might like it, but they don't want the upheaval and effort. They can't yet see your vision; they just see the chaos, challenges and effort that change requires. This means you need to be the warrior, the warrior fighting for your dream to become a reality. You will need to defend your vision and actions, but as a warrior, you keep going, and this forward motion helps you become transcendent.

Qualities of a warrior

As the warrior, you stand firm and even fight for your vision, taking action and breathing life into it until it becomes real. This stage requires immense courage so that you can keep moving forward, step by tiny painful step, or stride by giant flowing stride. If you don't stay committed, even in the face of seemingly insurmountable obstacles, you know your vision will never become real.

Every step you take leads by example, inspiring others to join the ranks of the bold and the fearless. You will have to draw on inner resourcefulness, strategy and cunning like never before to keep going, day after day. Now is the time for action, and you are the driving force forging the change the world awaits.

Transcendence

As a Transcendent, you are a changemaker. You'll be always working for the greater good. You exhibit autonomy and embrace complexity and creativity. You prioritise inner growth; you eagerly explore new experiences and seek a profound sense of purpose aligned with the greater good. You transcend ego and materialism, valuing selflessness and meaningful pursuits. Your peak experiences foster joy and unity with the universe, and you find fulfilment in the process of activities, inspiring and elevating those around you. You are always growing. You release attachment to outcomes. You passionately work to create a better world for all.

But it can be lonely. You have to deal with the scepticism of others. Few will *get* you. You will be constantly integrating new and profound insights. That's why, as a Transcendent, you know you have to keep moving and keep creating a better world, so you go around the cycle again. You stay conscious and transcend to higher and higher levels. We'll go into far more detail about the Transcendent in upcoming chapters.

Collective evolution: Seven stages to a conscious culture

The seven-stage cycle of evolution we've just described for an individual also applies to our collective culture. I observe that, as a species, we are at the liminal stage. We have reached the space between what was and what has yet to be. We have recognised that the world doesn't work and moved out of any denial. We've woken up and questioned who we are as a culture and species and how we live. We have been seekers and our quest for answers has revealed some uncomfortable truths. Yep, to paraphrase one of our culture's current changemaking popstars Taylor Swift: It's us. *We* are the problem. It's us.

But in this liminal stage, we just don't know what to change or how to do it. We are grieving and learning to let go. We know we can't go back to our old ways, but we don't have a vision or plan of where to go next (except, of course, now that you have this book, you do!). Knowing that we are all probably in the liminal stage does help though, because now we know what the next step is.

We need to create a collective vision of what we want our future to be like. We can all actively choose to participate in the collective creation of a conscious culture. We need the Transcendents to go beyond and lead us all into the unchartered future that no one has even considered yet. In the next chapter, we'll go into more detail about the qualities of a Transcendent and what this means for our conscious tipping point.

Summary

- Awakening is a journey of growth, experience and living, not a destination.

- The cycle of transcendent awakening consists of seven stages: harmoniser, awakening, seeker, liminality, visionary, warrior and transcendent.

- Each stage offers unique opportunities for growth and challenges to overcome.

- The cycle is a spiral of evolution, indicating continuous growth without a definitive endpoint.

- Both individuals and humanity as a collective undergo this cycle.

- As a collective we are all currently at the liminal stage, poised for our next awakening where we turn our collective vision into reality.

SELF-REFLECTION QUESTIONS FOR DEEPER EXPLORATION

1. How do you relate to the idea that life's purpose is to evolve and experience rather than reach a specific destination?

2. Can you identify your current stage in the cycle of transcendent awakening? What makes you think so?

3. Reflect on a time when you felt stuck in one of the stages. How did you move forward or what do you think could help you progress?

4. Considering the collective stage of humanity as being liminal, what vision do you have for our future? How can you contribute to realising this vision?

5. How does understanding the cycle change your perspective on personal and collective evolution?

10
The Transcendent Formula

To transcend means to go beyond. It's no longer enough to be a good person. It's not enough to be conscious, kind or nice. It's not enough to live a good life, it's not enough to do no harm. To transcend the meta-crisis and move our consciousness over the tipping point, we need to go further. We need to go beyond. We need to transcend the individual and move into the space of the collective where the needs of the many outweigh the needs of the one. Our Crown PowerCentre is our gateway to collective transcendence, to systemic change. This is what a Transcendent does. They transcend beyond. In this chapter, we'll craft a vision for the Transcendents: what they do and who they are not. You'll be guided by insights on how to become a consciously awakened and transcendent being.

How *not* to be a Transcendent

As wonderful as a Transcendent is, there seem to be some deeply unhelpful and damaging ideas about them, so let's clear those up. Here's what a Transcendent is *not*.

Perfect. A Transcendent isn't perfect; they are always striving to better themselves. They do not expect to be 'perfect'. They accept what is and change what they can. They seek feedback and constructive criticism to guide their growth and evolution. When we expect them to be perfect and without flaws, not only do we set ourselves up for disappointment but we set them up to fail as they will be forced to hide their human imperfections and try to create the illusion of perfection. This, of course, is unsustainable. We only have to look at the number of very good but equally imperfect humans who have been 'outed' simply for not being perfect.

Always kind, loving and 'nice'. Being a Transcendent means that you do what serves the highest good. This means sometimes doing things others don't want you to do, or not doing things that others do want you to do.

Always happy. A Transcendent can and *should* feel negative emotions. They know that emotions are their guidance system and to deny them is unhealthy and impractical. They understand that suppressing negative emotions leads to making bad choices and causes long-term emotional and physical health problems. Allow yourself to feel what you feel. Then, use those feelings to take action to change something, inside or out, to solve the cause of the emotions.

A 'yes-person'. A Transcendent can, and does, say no.

Arrogant. Transcendents are humble. A true Transcendent knows they are never 'done'. They fully understand that being a Transcendent means that they are constantly evolving. They aren't particularly interested in the opinions of others, so they don't feel the need to brag about or hide their talents.

'Done' and fully evolved. Evolution and enlightenment are infinite and a Transcendent knows this. To consider themselves 'finished' would deny them the source of their deepest fulfilment, which is to learn and grow.

Simplistic. There's a misconception that simply *being* awakened and conscious is enough and that the solutions to all our problems, individual and collective, are straightforward. Sometimes they are, but this is the exception rather than the norm. A Transcendent will usually reject binary thinking and simple, obvious solutions because they fully understand that complex situations demand complex understanding and nuanced solutions.

Now we know what a Transcendent is not, let's explore what a transcendent being *is* by looking at the qualities they embody.

Qualities of a Transcendent

Before you become overly obsessed with this list, it's important to note that no one quality is enough, nor is it essential that you have all of these qualities. Becoming transcendent is, most importantly, a journey, an approach, an attitude; it's not a destination. Many of the qualities interweave, overlap and relate to each other. Some qualities can't be fully actualised on their own; you can't have one without others.

Transcendence: To avoid the risk of implying that a Transcendent has achieved and embodies transcendence, let me clarify what transcendence means as a quality. The ability to experience and access transcendence goes beyond those 'bliss-fuck' states we discussed elsewhere. Transcendence refers to your ability to go beyond your own immediate concerns and connect with something larger than you.

However, it goes even further. Transcendence means a connection to something more, something higher, something spiritual. It might be a guide, a higher consciousness or your experience of the source. The name is irrelevant, but the experience of the support, love, guidance and connection that emanates from that connection to your source is as undeniable and powerful as it is indescribable. Transcendents have this access to their inner sorceress, mage or magician at the heart and soul of who they are.

Self-awareness: The journey to transcendence starts with an awareness of yourself. You know who you are; you know your purpose, your desires and needs, your strengths and your weaknesses. You are unafraid to explore the depths of who you are and regularly engage in self-reflection and exploration. You understand yourself as a constantly evolving individual without harsh judgement but with compassionate evaluation.

Expanded awareness and consciousness: You will always look beyond your personal and immediate concerns to understand the interconnectedness of all things. You are mindful of the impact of your actions and decisions on the greater whole.

Vision and imagination: A Transcendent is also a visionary. You see beyond the current reality and imagine a different future. You can see what is, here and now, but you also imagine what is possible. Your visionary imaginings may be far ahead of your time. You will use all your powers and other transcendent qualities to move towards creating your vision and building it into reality.

Unity and connection: You have a deep sense of oneness and interconnectedness with all beings and the environment. You can recognise that every individual, community and smaller system is part of a larger whole. You will seek to unite all. Your tools are collaboration, inclusiveness and compassionate understanding.

As a transcendent being, you have a deep sense of connection to something beyond the individual self. This might be a connection to the broader community, nature, the universe or a higher spiritual or moral dimension. Frequently, a Transcendent experiences this connection as being guided by your soul, spirit, source or higher evolved beings. Though this might sound as if it is bordering on madness or delusion, for a Transcendent, it's simply a gentle guiding presence offering reflections, insights and ideas, with a complete absence of any compulsion to obey or act on that guidance.

Divine: As a transcendent being, you know you are Divine. You have divinity within you, and you experience yourself as an aspect of the Divine by perceiving the unity in all life. When you have full awareness of your divinity, you no longer feel the need to strive, seek or yearn for it. It just *is*. It's who you are. You will seek to express your Divine nature and to be aware of the Divine in others. You stop seeing others as weak or in need of saving. Others' divinity will express itself uniquely, in its special way, so there is nothing to prove. You simply need to be yourself. If you know you are an aspect of God, you are infinite – just like God is – and so is everyone else.

When you truly accept your divinity, it becomes impossible to allow or perpetuate suffering. You know that you are not your pain. You are not your ego or your monkey mind. When you let go of your ego, you let go of any shame about your differences and perceived imperfections. You are not your body. You have a body, which you use to experience the physical world, but you *are* Divine.

Uniqueness: You are aware of your own unique, special self. You will authentically and unapologetically express your talents, abilities and even the qualities of being a Transcendent. You will have a distinctive and often unusual approach. You are unafraid and so will speak your truth, but you will do so compassionately.

Creativity: Your unique perspective and your willingness to explore, learn and experiment leads to an extraordinary ability to generate novel ideas, solve complex problems and make meaningful contributions to various fields. In whatever realm you explore, you will be the chef who creates a new dish from a fusion of unexpected flavours, the engineer who solves a chronic inefficiency in a production line, the poet who uses language in extraordinary ways... If you can imagine and dream it, you can embody it.

Independence and autonomy: You demonstrate a strong sense of autonomy and independence. You make decisions based on your values and beliefs rather than being excessively influenced by external pressures. You have the self-awareness necessary to fully understand your motivations, strengths and weaknesses.

Complexity: You have a rich and multifaceted inner life. Your default is to consider nuance and subtlety to explore and fully understand situations, problems, circumstances and causes. No knee-jerk, simplistic solutions for you! You will have a wide range of diverse interests, skills and perspectives, which you will draw on frequently. You engage with the world and others in a nuanced and thoughtful manner. This is how you can bring order to chaos. You are likely to be a polymath.

Differentiated: As a Transcendent, you develop unique qualities, thoughts and perspectives that set you apart from others. You are highly individual, unusual and unique. You do not need to follow the crowd, nor do you desire this. You dare to stand alone. You have a unique vision which you have arrived at after long and careful exploration.

Integrated: You have found ways to integrate the different aspects of yourself, including parts, approaches, perspectives, desired goals and actions. You are aware of the different parts of your inner world and find ways to create integration. Instead of rejecting parts that seem 'bad', you know they have a purpose for certain situations. You can see the bigger picture and understand different approaches, which leads to deep compassion, empathy and balanced decision-making as you can consider yourself, others and the whole.

Growth mindset: As a Transcendent, you prioritise your inner growth and personal improvement. You will consistently seek a deeper understanding of yourself and the world around you. You will also seek to learn new skills and gain new knowledge and understanding. Even if the training you seek doesn't immediately seem to have relevance to your role or problem, it gives you a breadth of experiences and approaches that can lead to unusual solutions (or it may have no obvious purpose whatsoever). Just as bench pressing doesn't seem to have an imme-diate application in the wider world, it increases muscle strength. Learning increases your ability to problem-solve in other areas. However, even this is a byproduct of the learning. You'll learn because you're curious. About everything.

Autotelic and joyful: You do things for the sheer plea-sure of doing them, not just to achieve a specific out-come or reward. You are fully engaged in the present moment, often experiencing flow, and find the activity itself to be rewarding and fulfilling. It's about finding joy and meaning in the process of an activity rather than solely focusing on the result.

Peak experiences are a feature of your intrinsic motivation and drive. A Transcendent accesses moments of intense joy, awe and a sense of oneness with the universe at will, and often. These experiences can be transformative and frequently leave you changed, as well as generating a greater sense of overall wellbeing, or they can simply be the driver for profound productivity.

As a Transcendent, you find lightness, joy and fulfilment in life. You can appreciate and embrace the pleasures of physical existence without losing sight of your spiritual connection, maintaining a playful approach to personal growth.

Purpose and altruism: You know who you are, what you're here to do and the gifts you bring to the world. This gives your life and work meaning beyond rewards, accolades and achievements. You're driven by intrinsic motivations rather than external incentives.

Your purpose comes not from what you'll get, but from what you can give. You enjoy doing what you do and knowing that others will benefit from it. You show a strong desire to benefit others and a genuine concern for their welfare.

Charisma and magnetism: At gatherings, you might have noticed you find yourself surrounded by people asking you questions, seeking your advice and yearning to bathe in the light of your presence and awareness. Your charisma might be loud and forceful, or it might be quiet and sensitive. It will likely vary according to time, place and circumstances. You tend to create an accepting and safe environment for others. While striving for the highest good, you understand when to offer support or encourage others to grow through challenges.

To some people, you will be magnetic. You create safe and accepting environments for others. Your charisma draws people to you. While striving for the highest good you understand when to offer support or encourage others to grow through challenges. Those who are transcendent will spot a fellow transcendent. Those who aspire to transcendence will be drawn to you and inspired by you.

Transcending ego and materialism: You can easily move beyond a limited focus on personal desires, material possessions and ego-driven motivations. You may even find it hard to relate to those who are driven by material outcomes for their own sake and find those who have this as their highest or main goal rather uninteresting. You recognise that their desire for status usually stems from an unmet emotional need which you have already fulfilled. Rather than judging or condemning those who have this desire, you are compassionate.

Summary

- Transcendence involves going beyond individual desires to serve the collective good.

- Being a Transcendent does not mean being perfect or nice all the time. A Transcendent embraces flaws and strives for progress over perfection.

- Transcendents experience and express a wide range of emotions, understanding them as a guide for action.

- Qualities of a Transcendent include an expanded awareness, creativity, autonomy, a growth mindset and a focus on purpose over material gains.

- A Transcendent navigates life with a deep sense of connection to others, the environment and a higher purpose, leveraging personal power for systemic change.

- The journey to becoming a Transcendent is marked by continuous learning, embracing complexity and fostering unity and diversity.

SELF-REFLECTION QUESTIONS FOR DEEPER EXPLORATION

1. Which of the qualities of a Transcendent do you feel you have access to? What stops you from accessing them more often?

2. Which of the qualities of a Transcendent are you yet to embody or access? Journal on some small steps you can take to start to find these within yourself.

3. How do you find the balance between kindness and assertiveness, especially when actions for the greater good might not align with others' wishes?

4. How do you experience uncomfortable or painful emotions? Do you try to repress and avoid them, or distract yourself?

5. Next time you feel uncomfortable emotions, rather than trying to 'stay positive', journal about what the emotions might be telling you. Are there actions you could take? Do you need to speak to another and ask them to change how they treat you, or how they behave towards other people?

6. In what ways do you nurture your vision for the future? Describe a vision you're passionate about bringing to life.

7. What is your life's purpose, and how does it contribute to the welfare of others? How do you use your gifts for the greater good?

8. Recall a moment when you consciously chose to put aside egoistic or materialistic desires for a higher cause. What was the outcome, and how did it influence your path towards transcendence?

11

The Architecture Of Ascension: The Pillars Of P.E.A.C.E.

When I started to become aware of the meta-crisis and the conscious tipping point, I became conflicted, wondering if personal and spiritual development were nothing more than a self-centred indulgence. Here we are in the eleventh hour, the eve of the bifurcation point, where our human culture and society will either evolve to a higher order or not. We'll transcend the meta-crisis or descend into something unimaginable and most likely horrific.

However, I no longer believe that to be true. As a leader who runs a business that supports other leaders who are guiding small and large groups at this pivotal time, one thing is clear. For leaders to do our best work, to be our most inspired, our most compassionate, visionary, brave and rational and to make choices that support the greater good, one thing is clear: we need to be emotionally regulated, supported, connected and well nourished. We need to have limbic systems that are far from being triggered into fight or flight or from being so perpetually triggered that our systems shut down. We need leaders who are physically cared for, well rested and replenished, have time and space to grow and envision, and are fully alive.

Becoming transcendent isn't something exclusive, only bestowed upon a chosen few like some random spiritual or genetic gift, or the luck of some mage who decides you're the *one*. Becoming transcendent is a choice and a calling. It's possible for anyone and everyone and requires a systematic process to become the most empowered, enlightened expression of who you are. In this chapter, I'll guide you through the map that will enable you to become the Transcendent you're choosing.

Pillars of P.E.A.C.E.

Transcendence begins with our inner work. A strong foundation of the following five strengths and skills is the start:

1. Purpose and meaning

2. Emotional resilience and Energy mastery

3. Autonomy and control

4. Connection to others

5. Enlightenment

Pillars of P.E.A.C.E.

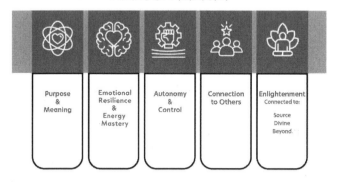

| Purpose & Meaning | Emotional Resilience & Energy Mastery | Autonomy & Control | Connection to Others | Enlightenment Connected to: Source Divine Beyond. |

Let's look at each of these in more detail.

1. Purpose and meaning

Many people mistakenly think of purpose in ways that are too specific or limiting. Your purpose is simple and, most importantly, it is dynamic. It will change and evolve throughout your life. At different times in your life, it will have a common core theme but may be expressed differently. Three components could be said to contribute to your purpose: Activities, Mission, People, which creates the acronym AMP. Amp is also the unit of current in electricity and relates to power.

- **Activities** are those tasks and actions that you love to do, that bring you joy, and that intrinsically and internally motivate you. When you engage in these activities, you lose all sense of time and enter into the flow state. This is a state where you are completely immersed in the activity, experiencing intense focus, involvement and enjoyment in the process without consideration of the result.

- **Mission** represents the impact, contribution or change you want to see in the world. Your mission could be what inspires you, or it could be what annoys you so much that you are driven to change it.

- **People** signifies the people you do your mission for or with. These might be your family or loved ones, or they might be those who you care about. I'd even go so far as to say that the people component might include animals.

With these three dialled in, you can begin to AMP up your purpose.

2. Emotional resilience and Energy mastery

Emotional resilience is key to being transcendent. When you live your purpose and seek to express it there will be challenges and setbacks. People won't like what you say or do and they'll tell you (and not always in a kind way). You need to have rock-solid emotional resilience and inner strength. Emotional resilience is what gives you the ability to bounce back from emotional pain, to strive through stressful times and to rise above adversity.

To access emotional resilience, you will need to have good emotional intelligence and be self-aware. You must have healed any trauma, released any limiting beliefs and have strategies and tools to continue doing this on an ongoing basis.

Energy mastery is your ability to access just the right amount and quality of energy at the right time. The ability to move between different energetic states to match the task, mood and environment is one of the defining features of a Transcendent. It gives them presence and charisma.

3. Autonomy and control

Autonomy and control are accessed by first taking huge personal responsibility. This means accepting the outcomes of your decisions, learning from them and then adapting your beliefs, actions and communication accordingly. Autonomy is empowering and stems first from self-esteem and confidence in your ability to learn from failure.

4. Connection to others

Being a Transcendent requires just the right amount of connection to others for the individual. Some people thrive from constant interaction with other people. For others, this will drain and deplete them. A Transcendent will need a good support network who will bolster you up, but also challenge your ideas to ensure you're making optimal choices and actions.

5. Enlightenment

This pillar refers to your ability to connect to whatever higher power or spiritual construct has meaning for you. You might access this within religion and you might not. It is personal and individual for everyone. You might think of it as a God or Goddess, or you might simply think of it as the best part of yourself, or it might be super consciousness, or maybe for you it is those highly evolved multidimensional beings from the future we were chatting with earlier. The important thing is that it's a state or level of awareness that you can access easily and which gives you guidance, insight, greater awareness, solace, comfort and a broader perspective on whatever situation you are facing.

For a Transcendent, enlightenment doesn't mean possessing any supernatural powers to perform miraculous feats. It is characterised by deep insights, profound connection to the world around us and being aware of the interconnectedness of all things. Enlightenment empowers you to live with intention, wisdom, harmony and clarity about yourself, your relationship to the world and your place in it.

If you want to be a Transcendent, or you know you already are and want to embody this even more, here are my suggestions on where and how to start (and continue) your growth.

Strengthening the pillars of P.E.A.C.E.

Now that we know what the pillars of P.E.A.C.E. are, let's consider ways we can strengthen them. I have intentionally kept this section of our book brief, only offering some signposts and suggested routes. To fully do justice to the evolution of the individual, we'd need libraries and most of the human knowledge in existence. Here, I want to give you an entry point, but with the caveat that this list is neither exhaustive nor even sufficient. I will make suggestions and I will fall short; there will be methods and tools that get missed here, which doesn't mean they aren't important or effective.

If you have tools that work to improve your emotional resilience, use them. You might consider trying others and that's entirely up to you. The motto of a Transcendent is, 'If it works, use it.' Here are some actions and tools that you might consider using.

Meditation and mindfulness: In all the history of spiritual and personal development and mental health, no tool is as foundational in its effectiveness to improve our psychological wellbeing as meditation.

If you meditate regularly, I encourage you to continue and even consider deepening your practice. If you have ever meditated and stopped, then I strongly encourage you to resume your practice. If you have never meditated before, then I urge you to start. You can find a free course on meditation on my website (www.cetfreedom.com). It offers a range of approaches and styles. Experiment with them and you'll find the optimal meditation practice for you.

Guided meditations to tap into your inner wisdom: Guided meditation, unlike unstructured meditation, enables you to consciously choose what changes might be installed in your unconscious mind. You can find, choose or create ones for yourself that enable you to create a deeper connection to your own inner wisdom, intuition and Higher Self.

Doing the deep inner work: Transcendence calls for the deep inner work. To go beyond superficial positive thinking or affirmations. To dive deep within to fully explore your hidden worlds. To heal anything that needs healing. To develop anything that needs developing. To grow what needs to be expanded. As a Transcendent, you will fearlessly and courageously look at all you might have repressed, denied or rejected and love, heal and grow it back to joy, wholeness and resilience. Being transcendent requires enormous emotional resilience and you bravely and tenderly do this for yourself.

Overcoming and deleting limiting beliefs: What we believe is real becomes real. What we believe is true becomes truth. What we believe is possible, we act on. What we believe is impossible becomes a hopeless reality. To change our reality, we need to act. To act we must believe there is a point to action. Nothing saps our energy, drive and will to act more than the limiting belief that 'there is no point.'

There are various tools to remove and delete limiting beliefs. Some of them include NLP, timeline therapy and hypnosis, to name a few. Conscious Emotional Transformation (CET) is one that I developed. If you have one that works, use it. I recommend CET because it is fast and comfortable for the client and practitioner. CET also uses the same principles of neuroplasticity that create trauma and instil beliefs in the first place. You can find out more about CET on my website. When we overcome our feelings of helplessness, we become empowered. When enough of us do this, we become unstoppable.

Reconnecting with nature: Nature is inherently soothing and calming to the nervous system. It regulates emotions, calms the limbic system and heals. It does this without effort; you can simply be in it and connect to it. You don't need to go into the Kalahari Desert – a walk in the park or a little light gardening will do. Go get muddy, get a bit wet or get hot and sweaty.

Embodiment: Yoga, tai chi, walking, working out, dancing, swimming, skiing, running… Do anything that moves your body to reconnect with yourself. Keep it fun and joyful and avoid making it a duty or chore. Become embodied.

Explore and reconnect with your spirituality: Whether through mystical tractions, organised religion or any spiritual practices, find your way back to your own Higher Self. Your Higher Self is the key to becoming transcendent. This is beyond a state; it is a way of being. When you are connected to your Higher Self, you go beyond ego and the individual. You become aware of yourself as infinite and part of something greater. This concept is so huge it would require several entire books to fully explain, but there are many resources on my website that might help.

Learn to access flow states: A flow state is a mental state when you are fully immersed in an activity, experiencing a heightened sense of focus, joy and engagement. Flow states are characterised by a balance of skill and challenge. You experience a loss of awareness of yourself because you are immersed in the task. Your performance is enhanced because you are focused on doing the task, rather than outcomes or anyone watching. You have profound positive feelings and time seems to stand still or fly by. You can experience flow states when you do almost anything, be it sports, writing, crafts or creating, but it usually requires an active component rather than being fully passive. For example, watching movies and reading are unlikely to trigger flow states, even though they are immersive. You usually leave a flow state with a sense of satisfaction and accomplishment. There is a whole science to accessing flow states for improving productivity (which is, yes, a little ironic, but the science makes it easier and removes the guesswork).

Develop critical thinking: Critical thinking enables us to analyse information and question assumptions. So much of what holds dysfunctional systems in place is the unconscious conditioning and manipulative messages that we are commonly subjected to. Critical thinking allows us to navigate complex issues, find what's really beneath the surface and inoculate our minds from manipulation. It starts by questioning underlying assumptions and seeking diverse perspectives. Actively seek out viewpoints that are different from your own. Read widely and critically from diverse texts. Practice problem-solving and logical reasoning. You might try puzzles and strategic games, or even explore real-world problems. Start educating yourself on logical fallacies, though you'll start to see them everywhere and that can become quite annoying (so I'm told). Keep an open mind and be open to changing your mind if, or when, you get new evidence. If you want others to change, you have to be willing to change yourself.

Find your tribe: As a Transcendent, you need support. As a Transcendent, it's easy to feel overwhelmed and isolated. You need to surround yourself with like-minded, supportive individuals – others who have a vision and want to be part of the solution rather than moan about the problems. Seek out others who deeply understand who you are and what you are working to achieve.

Be a seed crystal: A crystal grows from a tiny seed crystal. It's this that we must all be. The seed crystal for pure beautiful consciousness around which others will gather and form a bigger and bigger collective of pure crystalline consciousness. This is how we can all create change. Like a quartz cluster of brilliant diamond-like points, we shine our brilliance, reflect our love and form the foundations for change.

Summary

- Transcendence is accessible to anyone when they apply a systematic process to become the most empowered, enlightened version of themself.

- The pillars of P.E.A.C.E. – purpose and meaning, emotional resilience, autonomy and control, connection to others and enlightenment – serve as foundational pillars to support you in your journey to transcendence.

- Emotional resilience is vital for overcoming challenges, necessitating self-awareness, trauma healing and the release of limiting beliefs.

- Meditation and mindfulness are essential practices for improving psychological wellbeing and advancing spiritual development.

- Embodying the role of a 'seed crystal' is about inspiring change and leading others in the transformative journey towards a conscious culture.

SELF-REFLECTION QUESTIONS FOR DEEPER EXPLORATION

1. Consider each of the pillars in your life. Which ones are strong, and which are a little wobbly? Journal this and be compassionately honest with yourself.

2. What is your purpose? Do you know it? What are the activities? What's the mission? Who are your people?

3. What activities trigger a flow state for you? How can you create more opportunities for these in your life?

4. Describe a moment when you felt a deep sense of enlightenment or connection to a higher power. How did it guide your actions?

5. How do you cultivate critical thinking to challenge assumptions and make informed decisions?

6. Reflect on your support network. Do you have enough support? Is it the right kind of support? What additions to your support network would assist you in achieving your transcendent vision?

7. What steps could you take to be a 'seed crystal' for positive change in your community?

12

Overcoming Resistance On The Collective Journey To Transcendence

Aah, if only it was easy! We just decide to become transcendent and there we are. Only we don't, and we're not. In this chapter, we'll explore the idea that individual evolution and raising collective consciousness, rather than being in conflict, are two facets of the same crystal.

When a crystal is grown in a solution, it starts as a seed crystal suspended in a saturated solution. In the same way, a Transcendent is like a seed crystal initiating the growth of a larger structure. Each time our society shifted from one PowerCentre to the next, it began with a single individual with a single idea. This might have been so small that no one even noticed. However, as the idea grew and then spread as more people spoke about it, eventually the shift became inevitable.

We currently live in a dysfunctional world and the systemic, cultural and financial challenges negatively impact the mental health of many individuals. We know that we need to make changes to the whole, yet we often seem powerless to do so. Changing dysfunctional systems requires us to raise the collective consciousness, and to do that, we have to start by raising our consciousness. It starts with me. It starts with you. Sometimes the suggestions to raise consciousness to change the systemic problems put even more pressure on already exhausted and mentally fatigued Transcendents.

Overcoming inertia and gathering momentum

If you've ever ridden a bike, you will know that the first push of the pedal is the hardest. Once you're moving, pedalling becomes easy, almost effortless as you glide along. A common concept in engineering is the idea of resistance or friction. In the real world when we want to move something, build something or change something, there is always resistance or inertia. Inertia is the tendency of the body to remain at rest or continue to move in the same direction and speed (thank you, Newton).

Personal growth and societal transformation also involve inertia – the resistance to change. It's the comfort zone, the 'that's the way we've always done it' mindset. It's this closed mindset that refuses to consider another way. We all have it, and we must all overcome it, both individually and as a collective. This takes effort, energy and power. Hence the use of the word PowerCentre.

The good news is that once we start moving, momentum takes over and it becomes increasingly difficult to stop it or change direction.

And where we are as a collective, right now in the liminal phase where everything seems to be stuck or stopped, is perfect. It gives us time to reflect and pause so we can create the vision of what we want. Being mindful of our own and the collective inertia will help us choose the right course.

On the journey to transcendence, we will experience friction both from within ourselves (due to our personal inner resistance) and from the cultural ecosystem. The bigger the change, the more resistance there will be. It makes change harder but it also lets us know that it's worth it, because just the other side of resistance is energy and power.

Challenges to being transcendent

When you consider all those wonderful qualities of being transcendent, it might sound a little like being some kind of perfect, invincible, supreme being, with no cares in the world. Although there are many wonderful qualities about being transcendent, it also comes with its unique challenges. To fully prepare you for becoming a Transcendent, here are some of the challenges you might experience.

High expectations: Others may forget that you are still human and have unreasonably high expectations of you. They may demand more than you can reasonably give. Yes, as a transcendent being, you are strong and emotionally resilient, and because you exude that, sometimes others forget that you also have feelings and needs. Others assume you have all the answers.

As a Transcendent, you need to surround yourself with those as strong and compassionate as you are so you have somewhere you can show your human, vulnerable self and still be loved without the expectation of perfection. Find your tribe and your group. Find the place and people who will offer the same compassion and care that you give to so many.

The burden of strength: Because you inspire others with your inner strength, competence and capabilities, you might find that everyone expects you to be the strong one all the time. Others might dump all their problems on you, or expect you to be the saviour who fixes everything, without giving you so much as a word of thanks. It becomes expected, not respected. In business, families and organisations, those who demonstrate strength are often expected to carry others. You might find that your perfectly normal human failings are perceived as faults that are regularly accepted, tolerated and forgiven in others, but unforgivable and intolerable from you. There is a real sense that more is expected of you and less is forgiven.

You need to have crystal-clear boundaries and expectations from, and for, others. Taking on everyone's problems can also be disempowering for them. They won't learn how to solve their own issues. Take care that you don't end up carrying all the burdens, solving all the problems and doing all the work. You'll end up feeling resentful, and those around you will end up becoming codependent and disempowered.

Sharing wisdom effectively: If you have wisdom beyond the norm, it can be hard to communicate your wisdom and insights to others in a way that is understandable and relatable, especially when dealing with abstract or profound concepts. Sometimes it's better to stay silent until others are receptive and their minds are open to understanding new and radical concepts.

Getting hurt: Feeling hurt is a common occupational hazard for a Transcendent. We feel hurt when our gifts, wisdom, ideas and love are rejected by those we offer them to. The truth is, some will not understand your ideas, wisdom or gifts; they will view your offerings suspiciously and you may experience everything from a lukewarm reception to an aggressive rejection. I won't patronise you by saying, 'Try not to let it get to you,' or a similar platitude. Instead, I will honour and celebrate you for trying, for striving and for offering.

Balancing individual and collective needs: Finding a balance between your yearning to contribute to the greater good and taking care of yourself can feel almost impossible. As a Transcendent, you will have high expectations of yourself. Who's got time for a bubble bath and a massage when the world is burning and so many need your help? But this is exactly why you must take a bubble bath. You need to rest and replenish so you can rise even higher. You can't serve from an empty cup, so you must take time to find what fills yours and replenish it. Remember, despite all your amazing skills and qualities, you are still human and need rest, time and peace.

Loneliness: True Transcendents are rare. As a result, most people just won't *get* you or what you're doing. While they're pursuing material dreams or distracted by the daily gossip or grind, you're out there changing the world. This can cause you to feel isolated or disconnected from those who simply aren't at a similar level of awareness. For this and all the other reasons above, you must gather together with other Transcendents for support and advice, to vent, to heal, to learn from each other and to grow together.

The power of collective consciousness-raising

Hard as it might seem to change the trajectory of the entire planet, when it seems that everyone is asleep and oblivious to the dangers that await if we fail to change, never underestimate the power every one of us has. Just by reading this book and planting these seeds of possibility, your mind, or possibly a higher consciousness, will start to feed you ideas and inspiration for new ways of being and living.

There is a theory that to create change in a culture you only need 3.5% of the population to embrace these new ideas and concepts.[10] Collective manifestation has always played a crucial role in instigating and navigating societal shifts. As individuals, we have *some* power, but as a collective, we can become unstoppable. Here's how collective manifestation can influence our next major transition across the tipping point. As a species, we have the potential to:

- **Create shared intentions and visions:** When a large group shares a vision for the future and sends collective intentions, this unity can create a powerful force for change.

- **Amplify energy and focus:** When the energy of individuals is aligned towards a common goal, we create the potential for momentum and change. By clarifying our collective visions for a different future, we plant the seeds of this future.

- **Impress the field:** There's an esoteric theory that individuals and an aligned group can collectively create an energetic intention that increases the likelihood of the collectively imagined outcome. This may be no more than a theory – a little spicy psychology, or it may eventually be backed by evidence. Either way, a group of individuals each holding an unshakable belief in something becomes unstoppable. History shows this, as do our recent culture wars fuelled by fanatical ideologies. According to this esoteric concept, creating and amplifying a resonant field becomes like a thought form or thought virus (only a good one). When individuals and a group create a powerful vision, we impress the energetic field with our vision.

- **Turn thoughts into words; words become beliefs:** Beliefs guide and become actions. Repeated actions become habits. Habits become our automatic, subconsciously programmed way of living. If we all agree that an empowered conscious and transcendent culture is something worth desiring, then it's down to all of us to create it. Start with the energetics, the esoteric, the inner work. If all you have is your imagination, for today, that's enough.

- **Inspire and encourage collective action:** I've said that Transcendents are charismatic and magnetic. When we apply these traits towards the shared vision of a conscious culture, we can serve as inspirations for others to do the same.

- **Develop hope, purpose and connectedness:** If hope is all we have, then let us hope – and hope hard. Hope is a force. If we hope for more consciousness, then let each of us consciously create consciousness. By hoping, we will trigger spiritual and psychological changes.

- **Create new cultural narratives:** Write a new story for humanity's future. Write it. Speak it. Share it. Repeat it again and again. Make the story of a future-conscious culture the default. The norm. Make it inevitable. Make it so unsurprising that we can't imagine it *not* to be true. Keep telling this story as if it is a foregone conclusion.

Collective consciousness raisers meet the collective shadow

There are those of us (you, my darling reader, are one) who are aware that raising consciousness is the answer. There are those of us who aren't gurus and don't want to be, but who are choosing to be part of the solution and no longer perpetuate the problem. There are those of us who are actively choosing to raise consciousness and to become Transcendents.

And what happens when we do this? We will bring the collective into an awareness of their own pain. An awareness of the harsh and painful truth that we, too, have contributed to systemic problems. Not because we're evil, but because we were conditioned by that system. As we come along, shining the light on the collective unconscious, we're bound to meet the collective shadow. The collective shadow is a consciousness that has no therapeutics; it has massive guilt and shame, and there we are, shining our light and bringing it into awareness. What happens?

The collective shadow wants to stay hidden. It will defend its darkness. It will resist. If you have been striving and struggling, trying to bring your light to the world only to find that the world would rather stay in darkness, know that you are not alone. And if you haven't experienced this resistance yet, here are some of the ways that you might:

- **Cultural resistance:** The current prevailing culture and accepted societal norms refuse to accept your ideas.

- **Market resistance:** People don't buy the services or products which would raise consciousness or support the adoption and implementation of your ideas. This is common for entrepreneurs when they hit consumer scepticism or reluctance.

- **Psychological resistance:** Individuals or groups simply don't believe you; they reject your ideas and refuse to even consider or contemplate your ideas. They will frequently demonstrate cognitive biases, prejudice and fear of change.

- **Psychic resistance:** An internal, often instinctive, unconscious resistance that emerges in response to change. It might present as mental blocks, gut reactions and emotions such as fear, dread, anxiety or generalised, unexplained reluctance. It can appear entirely energetic and intangible.

- **Technological resistance:** The technology to support your idea simply hasn't been invented yet. Babbage invented the first computer, but until semiconductors came along, it wasn't much use.

- **Authority/power resistance:** The established power dynamics within a group, organisation or civilisation are threatened by your new ideas or highly competing interests.

- **Institutional resistance:** Corporations, organisations or government entities resist change due to bureaucratic inertia, regulations and entrenched norms.

- **Ideological resistance:** This resistance originates from political groups, formal and informal, due to conflicting values, beliefs and ideologies.

- **Theological resistance:** This opposition stems from conflicts of faith, doctrine and dogma. People might perceive you or the work you're doing as 'evil'.

- **Environmental resistance:** The immediate, natural world and environment can resist a new idea. This resistance can show up even when your work involves sustainable development or ecological interventions.

- **Energetic resistance:** Energetic resistance is the most frustrating and distressing. It can even make you feel as if you are cursed. Subtle, intangible energy resists your efforts to raise consciousness.

If you've experienced any of these kinds of resistances, rest assured that you are not cursed, even if it feels like it! But you do need support. This is where groups are so important. Conscious communities and collectives that have nonjudgemental therapeutics can support you.

Know or find your role – you don't have to do it all

During the writing of this book, I got crippling writer's block many times. It was a combination of the pressing urgency I felt to get this message out, and because of the desire to offer an answer to the meta-crisis. I found myself obsessively trying to learn about financial systems, politics, big tech and big pharma. However, during a meditation when I asked my higher consciousness questions to help me move forward, I received a profound realisation.

I don't have to do it all. I don't have to come up with a solution to every problem. That's not my role. It's not my role to create a new financial system that's more equitable. Perhaps it's yours. It's not my role to challenge inequality and racism. Perhaps that's yours. It's not my role to change the education system or build an alternative. Perhaps that's yours. My role, right now, is to write this book. To show the patterns. To offer some hope and a little guidance. My role is to show others that together, we evolve and awaken as a species. My role is to facilitate transformation and growth and to assist leaders in moving past their inner friction and resistance. My role is to create spaces and welcome people into our groups, supporting the Transcendents to perform their roles. To offer sounding boards and places where we can have discussions that might be unfavourable elsewhere. Where we can ask the unanswerable questions and contemplate the un-contemplatable. To consider, explore and experiment, even if it's only with our thoughts.

Your first role is the first pillar of P.E.A.C.E. – finding what your role or purpose is. You need to find what your part might be in moving humanity across the tipping point to create a conscious culture.

Summary

- **We're all in this together:** Starting with you and me, sparking a big change is all about each of us stepping up our game. It's like being that tiny crystal that gets a whole bunch of others to join in and grow something amazing.

- **The first steps are the toughest:** Kicking off any change is super hard, but once you get rolling, it's like riding a bike downhill.

- **When things push back, push forward:** If you're feeling pushback, it means you're onto something big. It's not easy, but it's worth it.

- **Transcendents have it tough, too:** Being a transcendent isn't all sunshine and rainbows. Expectations are sky-high, and juggling your needs with the world's needs can be a tightrope walk.

SELF-REFLECTION QUESTIONS FOR DEEPER EXPLORATION

1. Think of some ways you could personally contribute to raising collective consciousness. What are some small steps you could start with that might make an impact, even if it's tiny?

2. In what ways have you experienced inertia or resistance in your own journey, and how have you overcome it?

3. How can you support others in overcoming their resistance to change and fostering a more collectively conscious community?

4. Reflect on a time when you felt like a 'seed crystal' initiating change. What did you learn from this

experience, and how can it inform your future actions?

5. Considering the challenges faced by Transcendents, how can you ensure you maintain your wellbeing while striving for collective improvement?

Conclusion

THEOSS's ultimate activation: Unity consciousness

So, here we are at the end of this current cycle in the Project THEOSS: The Evolution of our Species and Society. We began with the story of the activation of humanity's collective PowerCentres, so let's start our ending there.

The last PowerCentre in the system is the Crown PowerCentre, the gateway to transcendence and universal consciousness. We have yet to activate this PowerCentre, but we are at the tipping point. What can we expect when we collectively activate the highest PowerCentre?

We can expect to herald an era of integration and enlightenment. We will transcend not only our individual egos but the collective ego of our species. Until now, we have considered ourselves more important, more intelligent and all-around better than all other species. Perhaps AI shows us that we might not be. As we begin to experience higher states of consciousness that enable us to transcend our individual consciousness so that we are aware of not only our own thoughts but the interconnected thoughts, feelings and ideas of all beings, the universe itself is no longer an abstract or intellectual idea. It becomes our lived reality.

As each of the lower PowerCentres activated, the excess of the lower one moved into a state of balance. A healing took place. We now need to heal *all* of our collective traumas. This means we heal our own traumas and honour and heal others' traumas. Everyone's pain is the pain of the whole. This would eliminate the need for trauma competition (I had it worse than you! I'm in more pain than you!).

Imagine how a mother, seeing her child in pain, feels pain because of the love she feels for her own offspring, a precious part of herself. This is what we will experience when we see *all beings* as no longer apart from us, but a part of us; we will all feel the collective pain and joys of all. We will recognise that pain is pain and to heal you is to heal me; to heal them is to heal us.

We will transcend duality, moving us out of a 'them versus us' mentality and into the experience of unity. The divisions of the excesses of the lower PowerCentres will become so extreme as to allow us to horseshoe our consciousness around in a similar way to the ideologies of the left and right that have been and are taking place in the present culture wars.

The activation of the Crown PowerCentre is a collective spiritual awakening, but it's not about pursuing individual, material gains or 'cool' spiritual powers, which came with the excess of our collective Third Eye PowerCentre. At this level, spiritual awakening is all about seeking and achieving a deeper meaning, purpose and connection to the whole of humanity and the cosmos.

The Crown PowerCentre has the perfect balance of emotion and reason. The overactive heart no longer overshadows facts with feelings. It's not facts or feelings, but both. Critical thinking *and* discernment; truth *and* wisdom. Feelings become facts that have not yet been revealed or understood, and facts explain why we might feel a certain way.

The excesses of the Solar Plexus PowerCentre (greed and excessive individualism) and the Sacral PowerCentre (degradation of excess energy) remind us of the need for our collective responsibility to prioritise the wellbeing of the community, the ecosystem *and* the planet. The excesses of the Base PowerCentre with its overly rigid systems and structures show us the need for stable foundations *alongside* the flexibility of the Sacral PowerCentre, which allows us to adapt and change and to apply what works and what is useful, rather than blind adherence to rules.

We approach the activation of the collective Crown PowerCentre with a vision of a future where harmony, peace and spiritual fulfilment guide our actions and intentions. Individuals and communities will have roles to play in this transformation. It starts with inner work. It starts with raising one's consciousness. It continues towards a time of collective rituals, meditations and actions that embody our highest aspirations.

The activation of the collective Crown PowerCentre is both an end and a beginning. It is the culmination of the lessons learned through the challenges and excesses of the lower PowerCentres, ushering in the dawn of a new era of consciousness and enlightenment. As we navigate this transition, we have a beautiful opportunity to reimagine what it means to be an evolving human.

Epilogue

Ending this book has been hard. It's hard for me personally, because I hate goodbyes. You hang up. No, you hang up first. Bye. See you. Oh, before you go... Now, you hang up. Love you. Bye...

It's hard because we are not at the 'end' yet. Indeed, to want to get to any kind of end would seem to be nothing less than wishing for our own ending. In our fairy stories, the hero slays the dragon. Harry slays Voldemort in wand-to-wand combat. Frodo returns to the shire triumphant. Neo is whirling about in the sky. Those endings seem easy and natural.

But the truth is, we are not there yet, and that's the point of this story. We are not at the end. To avoid racing towards our end, we need this book. Project THEOSS does not end – only our current cycle does. This is both an ending and a beginning, but this is not *the* end.

Afterword:
From Lisa With Love

Challenging, crazy times, complicated messages and global confusion... Could this be what you have been training for your whole life? Maybe *you* are the person the world is calling for right now. Maybe *you* have exactly what your community needs. I celebrate all of you changemakers, doing what you're called to do. Staying strong. Connecting with your brilliance.

I invite you to stay connected to this work. To me. To us. Keep the conversation going. Keep embodying emotional resilience and doing the inner work to stay that way. Drawing on your talents and skills to live your purpose. Being the *one* for those who are looking to you right now.

I see you. I know you're doing this. I celebrate you. I love you.

Resources And Further Reading

Writing this book involved significant research and reading about these topics. If you want to explore any of these themes further, we have created an online list of books, articles, podcasts and other resources to explore. We add to it regularly as we continue to research this theme.

You can find a list of resources and further reading at www.OCTPBook.com.

Notes

1 K Kowalski, 'A Crisis of Crises: What is the meta-crisis?' (SLOWW, no date), www.sloww. co/meta-crisis-101, accessed 18 April 2024
2 Dr L Turner, *I Loved a Paedophile: The seduction, abduction and liberation of a life* (CreateSpace Independent Publishing Platform, 2013)
3 Dr L Turner, *CET Yourself Free: Change your life with the gentle alchemy of Conscious Emotional Transformation* (Rethink Press, 2022)
4 J Redfield, *The Celestine Prophecy* (Warner Books, 1993)
5 ND Walsch, *Conversations with God: An uncommon dialogue Book 1* (Hampton Roads, 1995)
6 L Balita-Centeno, 'How Social Media Is Making You Sad, According to Science' (MUO,

19 November 2020), www.makeuseof.com/
social-media-making-you-sad-scientific-studies,
accessed 19 April 2024

7   N Sherman, 'Purdue Pharma to plead guilty in
$8bn opioid settlement' (BBC, 21 October 2020),
www.bbc.co.uk/news/business-54636002,
accessed 19 April 2024

8   L Balita-Centeno, 'How Social Media Is Making
You Sad, According to Science' (MUO, 19
November 2020), www.makeuseof.com/social-
media-making-you-sad-scientific-studies,
accessed 19 April 2024

9   Dr L Turner, *CET Yourself Free: Change your life
with the gentle alchemy of Conscious Emotional
Transformation* (Rethink Press, July 2022)

10 D Robson, 'The "3.5% rule": How a small
minority can change the world' (BBC Future,
14 May 2019), www.bbc.com/future/
article/20190513-it-only-takes-35-of-people-to-
change-the-world, accessed 19 April 2024

Acknowledgements

J ust as the evolution of our society and species is a journey, writing this book has been a similar adventure, and I have been fortunate enough to have many travelling companions accompanying, supporting, guiding, navigating and carrying snacks along the way.

First, to my husband, John Turner, my steadfast supporter through every high and low, and provider of snacks – your unwavering belief in my dreams fuels my courage to pursue them.

To Dr Jennifer Reimer, or lovely Jenn, who was more than an editor but rather a writing coach – thank you for helping to bring my words to life and translating my random ideas into something readable and resonant. Your skill in refining my thoughts has made this book possible. Thank you also for your endless patience while my ideas ran down rabbit holes in random directions and you gently brought them back to the core message of the book.

To my incredible team, whose support and encouragement have been indispensable. Each one of you plays a crucial role in this shared mission, and I am deeply grateful for your commitment and enthusiasm.

To Laura, my head coach, whose dedication has lightened my load in ways I couldn't have imagined. Your guidance has been an integral part of my ability to focus on the book.

A special thank you also goes to Elizabeth Purvis who encouraged me to extend the reach of this work into the energy field. Your insight and foresight have opened new pathways for this book's journey.

I would also like to extend my gratitude to several key figures who have inspired and supported me in the background:

To my mentors, who have guided me with their wisdom and shared invaluable lessons not only on spirituality but in life.

To the countless workshop participants and readers who have shared their transformations and insights with me, enriching my understanding and purpose. Everyone who listened to my explanation of the Project THEOSS model and asked questions has helped to shape and guide this book. It was *you* who told me what needed to be said – even if it was through blank stares and confused looks.

To the community of visionary leaders, conscious leaders, transcendents and changemakers who continue to inspire and drive the global conversation on conscious evolution. You are who we have been waiting for and I celebrate everything you do towards reaching the goal of making this world better for all.

Last, my deepest thanks go to you, the reader. Your engagement and openness to exploring new dimensions are what make this work truly meaningful.

By reading this book, you are raising consciousness and doing the work. Keep thinking, questioning and talking about this to create a legacy of transformation. Thank you for joining me on this remarkable journey. Let's keep travelling.

The Author

Dr Lisa Turner is a leading voice in the spiritual community, the bestselling author of CET *Yourself Free* and a passionate advocate for humanity's conscious evolution. Uniting her academic contributions along with her spiritual training, she has helped thousands of people around the world to connect with their Higher Self in ways that offer grounded, practical approaches by integrating clear, actionable steps into their daily lives.

Her psycho-spiritual technology, Conscious Emotional Transformation (CET), has seen success within the military in treating PTSD, and with politicians, business leaders and entrepreneurs in assisting in achieving greater success with ease.

Lisa is a published author of five books, one of which is currently being developed for the screen.

Lisa lives in Cornwall where she spends her days walking on the coast or the moors, swimming, knitting and baking for her family.

- www.cetfreedom.com
- www.facebook.com/cetfreedom
- www.linkedin.com/company/cetfreedom/
- www.instagram.com/cetfreedom/
- twitter.com/DrLisaTurner
- www.tiktok.com/@drlisaturner